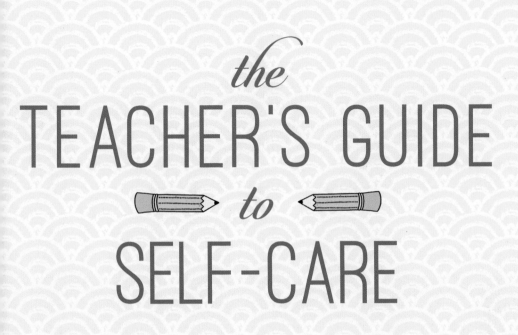

the

TEACHER'S GUIDE

to

SELF-CARE

the
TEACHER'S GUIDE

to

SELF-CARE

THE ULTIMATE CHEAT SHEET FOR THRIVING THROUGH THE SCHOOL YEAR

MELANIE J. PELLOWSKI
author and educator

Skyhorse Publishing

Skyhorse Publishing books may be purchased in bulk at special discounts for sales promotion, corporate gifts, fund-raising, or educational purposes. Special editions can also be created to specifications. For details, contact the Special Sales Department, Skyhorse Publishing, 307 West 36th Street, 11th Floor, New York, NY 10018 or info@skyhorsepublishing.com.

Skyhorse® and Skyhorse Publishing® are registered trademarks of Skyhorse Publishing, Inc.®, a Delaware corporation.

Visit our website at www.skyhorsepublishing.com.

10 9 8 7 6 5 4 3 2 1

Library of Congress Cataloging-in-Publication Data is available on file.

Cover design by Daniel Brount
Cover illustrations by Melanie J. Pellowski

Print ISBN: 978-1-5107-5795-0
Ebook ISBN: 978-1-5107-5796-7

Printed in China

To my dad, Michael, for teaching me to tackle life's challenges through lessons learned on the softball field, and encouraging me to pursue professional happiness through a well-rounded, creative career.

Table of Contents

A Note for Teachers

"Teachers are heroes."
—Casey, teacher

If you want to become a better person, be a teacher. We might not have all realized this when signing up to pursue a career in education, but this job inevitably makes us better people. It reminds us to be patient, polite, and understanding. It instills a sense of character, respect, and community that isn't always present in every other profession. The schedule encourages us to succeed in every avenue of life, not just at work.

In order to guide children, we are compelled to represent traits of quality on a daily basis. Not just when we stand in front of students in our classrooms, but when we stand in front of anyone on any given day. There's a certain pride that comes with being a teacher. It isn't just a job. It's a duty and a way of life.

THE MANY ROLES OF TEACHERS

Not to toot our own horns, but anyone who has been in a classroom knows that teachers can do anything we put our minds to. We're crafty, creative, and compelled to grow. The title of teacher is one that encompasses many roles; we might not be great at all of them, but we do our best. On any given day, we harbor every emotion out there. It's our job to teach students book smarts, but a more important mission is to impart values and common sense. Were they inspired? Did they build confidence? Did they learn something that they can apply in the real world? We answer their questions all day long, and we ponder our own once the day is done.

Teaching isn't a job for everyone. It takes a certain level of finesse, talent, and personality to be able to perform well as a teacher. Geniuses who are great at their discipline in the professional world might not be as comfortable transferring that knowledge to others in a classroom setting. Sure, we have the summers off, but any teacher will agree, the long breaks are required for us to remain sane, healthy,

and functional as human beings. We cram a year's worth of work into ten months. That's why we're exhausted by the time the sun is beating down on our rosy cheeks!

THOSE WHO CAN DO IT ALL, TEACH

Not just anybody can walk through the door of a classroom and be a good teacher. It takes practice, hard work, and most of all, a patient ability to communicate with all kinds of people. The best teachers carry a versatile set of skills; an ability to do the work in the real world and a knack for explaining how they did that work to others. Yes, the work of an educator is fulfilling, rewarding, and full of perks—but it's certainly no walk through the park.

The beauty of teaching is that it affords professionals the ability to pursue their own passions outside of the classroom. We can be dedicated and invested in our jobs as educators, while still enjoying the chance to explore our own personal interests outside of school. Some of our hobbies might include taking bubble baths. (Hey—no judgment there. We deserve it!)

In the outside world, teachers are scientists, mathematicians, writers, artists, musicians, and mechanics, and our roles don't stop there. We're all kinds of dreamers, and none of our personal stories are the same. Many of us have side jobs to fulfill a hobby or make ends meet. Some of us loved the classroom and stayed there. Others found their way back. There's no one path to becoming a

teacher. The important thing is that we're here now, and we're doing it. We have the chance to help others thrive, and in doing so, we hold the blueprints to build a good life all around.

> "I have always considered teaching as a career. It runs in the family. My mother, aunt, brother, and many cousins are teachers as well."
> —Corrin, teacher

TEACHERS ARE TIMELY

Teachers are not only educators. Some of us are experts in our fields, and some of us are honestly just experts at putting on a good show. After all, teaching is a daily performance where we sometimes have to go off-script. Standing in front of a group of modern-day students with technical distractions glowing in the palms of their hands is only part of our challenge. Times change, and there are constantly new hurdles. Digital documents have replaced penciled lesson plans. Report cards aren't mailed—they're uploaded. In spite of all of the technology and all of the social changes, one thing remains constant. Teachers are valuable assets in the future of education.

> "I enjoy giving back. Education is a powerful tool that can change the future."
> —Casey, teacher

TAKING CENTER STAGE

Okay, so we aren't performing heart surgery, but we are constantly performing, and our hearts are typically full. (Yes, even if that one annoying kid makes us feel guilty for envisioning karma coming back to haunt him in ten years.) We can't just show up on days that we are tired and slug through four cups of coffee with our heads down. We have to actually show up, smile, and be ready to give a presentation. We might be going on stage without hair and makeup (who has time for that?) but all eyes are on us whether we feel like performing in front of others or not. Some days, we may as well be lion tamers. Other days, we are therapists. We learn to rely on our own intuition to assess whether we are having a successful day. This

might mean something different to everyone. Some teachers just try to get through material without any kind of disciplinary distraction. Other teachers search for joyful expressions on the faces of students building confidence and friendship while exploring creative ideas. Some teachers encourage high-level thinkers to ponder outside the box; others help slow learners overcome obstacles.

> "The most fulfilling aspect of my job is taking the student in my class who has the behavioral problem or is low functioning academically and having them realize that they have the ability to succeed. Watching their eyes light up or having them crack a smile because they realize their potential is the greatest gift. Acknowledging the ones who struggle and showing them the door to success is open for them too does wonders for your classroom."
> —Kristen, teacher

THE GOOD LIFE

Knowing your classroom and your role there is the first step to understanding how you can be your own kind of successful. It's important for us to be able to utilize the work and accomplishments of our colleagues for inspiration while still defining our own goals and not comparing apples to oranges. We can always learn something new, but what works for one  classroom setting might not work for another. Just as each student's path to learning is different, individual teachers may thrive on their own unique definition of success.

We aren't just helping our students learn something new. We are exposing ourselves to a challenging process where, each and every day, we too aim to grow and become better. This goes for outside the classroom as well. While we write lesson plans, inspire future generations, and organize our lives at work, let's do our best not to forget about the other good stuff that makes us whole. We're good people and, by golly, we deserve the good life.

Top Ten Back-to-School Songs

"ABC" by The Jackson 5
"Beauty School Dropout" by Frankie Avalon
"School Days" by Chuck Berry
"What a Wonderful World" by Sam Cooke
"Baba O'Riley" by The Who
"Rock 'n' Roll High School" by the Ramones
"Another Brick in the Wall" by Pink Floyd
"Don't Stand So Close to Me" by The Police
"Welcome to the Jungle" by Guns n' Roses
"I Will Survive" by Aretha Franklin

Chapter 1

BACK TO SCHOOL

Every teacher knows that no student is the same as any other. Students come from different backgrounds. They have unique personalities. They require a certain type of finesse in the delivery of information. They learn differently, they communicate differently, and they respond differently. Some students prefer to learn a lesson by seeing something. Others need to hear the lesson, or write it down. Some kids are hams and can take a joke. Others take every word to heart. It's our job to assess and understand how to connect with different types of students while not making any of them cry by accident. We aim to spread joy, not sarcastic undertones (even if they are irresistible and funny).

TYPES OF TEACHERS

We weren't born yesterday, and we were once young students ourselves. Growing up hasn't changed our special human dynamic. We are unique individuals who thrive at multitasking and making the best out of a bad day. So what if we spill coffee on ourselves every single morning? We're all kind of a mess, but some of us are better at hiding it. We share a lot in common as teachers, but there are also defining characteristics that make us who we are as people.

THE OVERACHIEVING TEACHER

We all have a little bit of overachiever in us. For some, it's lying dormant. We hide it away underneath other layers of self-care or self-destruction. For others, it's on the forefront of accomplishment in every avenue of life, thus setting the bar high for other teachers and annoying every last one of us. It's great to be ambitious and to care about the quality of your work, but the overachieving teacher takes goal-setting and go-getting to a whole new level. The kings and queens of every extracurricular activity, overachievers don't mind sacrificing their free time to work with students or help others. Their grades are done on time, their lesson plans are on point, and their classrooms smell like lavender or some other kind of perfect. Overachievers tend to be awesome people, too, which makes it difficult to hate them. Don't worry, slackers. The nature of balance in the universe requires that underachieving folks be somewhere on the staff roster, too.

THE SLACKER TEACHER

Slacker teachers might be overachievers in the real world, but in the teaching world, they appear lazy or disorganized. That's because most teachers are on top of everything. Slacker teachers? Not so much. Slacker teachers are the reason we can't have nice things. They require administrative hand-holding to be productive. They rarely post lesson plans, sometimes dress like students, and online shop during their prep periods. They chitchat during staff meetings (that is, if they even show up), and they always ask to borrow a pen. We all have a little bit of slacker in us; the key is to keep it at bay. Otherwise, we might gain twenty-five pounds before summer or lose our stamina to succeed during the school year. Slacker teachers are careless about a lot of things, but that doesn't mean they don't care about kids. In fact, they might be the teachers who care the most.

THE HOT-MESS TEACHER

Hot-mess teachers are easily the most relatable, easygoing, and forgiving members of the staff. They make a sincere effort to be punctual and productive in spite of boarding the struggle bus every morning. Hot-mess teachers sleep through their alarms. They occasionally forget to brush their hair. They often call the main office in a panic because they are stuck in traffic. These deranged but lovable unkempt delinquents are a breath of fresh air. They creatively mask their inner bundle of tiny failures (like forgetting to fill up their gas tank or pack a lunch) with an optimistic outlook, sharing an affinity for helping random strangers and stray dogs. While others try to display a more polished version of themselves to the rest of the staff, hot-mess teachers unapologetically shout, "This is me!" They are a walking reminder that life is a journey, not a destination. They give students the confidence that they too can find a job someday.

THE SPIRITED TEACHER

Spirited teachers are the life coaches and cheerleaders of the teaching staff. They wake up in a good mood and somehow they stay that way—all day. A crowded parking lot, broken copy machine, and moody class of children are no match for their positive attitudes. Their divine energy lights up a room and lights a fire under every other lazy bum who works alongside them. Spirited teachers are the first to represent their school's colors on spirit days and they are a walking advertisement for the school store. They have a secret handshake with the school mascot (or they secretly are the school mascot). Their classroom is likely displaying every motivational quote known to man and it's either written in glitter or school colors. Sometimes, an encounter with a spirited teacher is the afternoon pick-me-up every other normal person needs to make it through the rest of the day.

THE SPORTY TEACHER

Sporty teachers don't have to teach gym to spend their afternoons hitting the gym. They maintain a strong and slim figure in spite of a hectic work schedule that drains their insides, living their best lives in athletic sneakers and sweat-resistant T-shirts. Most of the time, they're eating well and getting rest. They know how to do it all and they don't even have bags under their eyes. Apparently, the exhaustion of being a teacher doesn't affect their superhuman blood cells in the same way. That, or they're juicing on multivitamins and kale-based diets. Sporty teachers have a healthy glow about them. They are bundles of energy and joy. While everyone else struggles to reach for a gallon of ice cream and the TV remote at the end of the school day, they're putting in miles and making it look like a piece of cake.

THE SMARTY-PANTS TEACHER

All teachers know something about something, but smarty-pants teachers think they know everything about everything. They are a walking encyclopedia and every school's best shot at finding fame on *Jeopardy!* While thorough, smarty-pants

teachers are sometimes too consumed with information to realize their presentation may need a little more finesse. They might linger too long after a conversation has ended or respond to an emotional situation in a robotic way. In spite of all of this, they are kind, well-intended, and totally awesome at trivia. Forget about their socially awkward external layer, these reincarnated Einsteins are blessed with hearts of gold. Not to mention, their brain power comes in handy during emergencies and oddball situations. They know just what to do when weird stuff hits the fan.

THE POPULAR TEACHER

Popular teachers are all about positive messaging. They might be people-pleasers, but they aren't pushovers. They connect with kids on a human level and don't talk down to students. Rather, they hold conversations with students. These well-liked, charismatic pillars of the community tend to be parental favorites. They know how to present facts in ways that leave everyone at a meeting feeling heard, accomplished, and valid. They exaggerate what's good and politely mention what needs improvement. They excel at building relationships and genuinely care about other people's feelings. Popular teachers have to be careful because some students may try to take advantage of their forgiving and pleasant personalities. The most successful teachers remain popular in spite of students knowing they can't get away with everything.

THE OLD-SCHOOL TEACHER

Old-school teachers are stuck in their ways, and that's not to say that their ways are better or worse than what's fresh and new in education. These old chaps might have a chip on their shoulder or they might carry the weight of the school on their shoulders. They take pride in their work and wear that badge of honor on their sleeves. They put in their time so they no longer have the time of day to put up with anybody else's frivolous poppycock. Old-school teachers love talking about what life was like back in their day. They've experienced social and cultural changes the rest of us have only read about in history books. Their anecdotal tales are often inconceivable and embellished but still informative and thoughtful. Like lovable but kooky grandparents at a holiday gathering, old-school teachers are a part of every staff family. They've been through every district initiative and lived to tell about it.

THE CRAFTY TEACHER

Crafty teachers are keen and ambitious creatives who view their classroom walls as a blank canvas open to interpretation. They tend to love movies, music, and popular culture. First to crack a joke during an awkward silence, you can count on crafty teachers to make sure their quip is sensitive to all audiences. Crafty teachers are mysterious open books who thrive in the restricted section of the library. They create a professional image that they prefer to uphold at all times, which is why they duck behind produce when spotting a student at the grocery store. They are passionate about their teaching careers but experts at crafting a balance. They tend to fly under the radar. Instead of making waves, they make crafts and classroom décor. They give their professional life everything they have during contract hours, and then they depart down a path of mystery. They are clever, confident, and quite good at setting boundaries.

THE TYPICAL TEACHER

The truth is that a typical teacher pulls a few traits from every type of teacher. Being versatile is important for educators, as we never know what kind of situation we will be dealing with in the classroom. While it's fun to reflect on personality traits of different teachers, typically, none of us can be generalized as one type of teacher. Our "type" might change with our mood. Our tolerance for putting up with other people's hogwash really depends on the day. Most of the time, we are just trying our best. Then, we go home, get some rest, and do it all over again.

> "I think a great teacher is someone who inspires students to believe in themselves and is always evolving."
> —Nicole, teacher

We are all ambitious until we realize we can't keep up with every single goal we set at the start of the school year. We make and break fitness goals or dodge pep rallies because we're just out of steam. We may slack on Monday and become a hot mess by Wednesday. We can be smart in our own subjects and we can be socially awkward, too. We're all in the same boat, which is why we should give one another a break when we see a colleague just trying to make it through the day.

We should give ourselves a break, too, when that "perfect" coworker seems to be doing everything right. Behind their classroom door, they are probably struggling to put on a good show.

> "I struggle with people who do not share my sense of urgency. I try to motivate them. Sometimes I am successful, sometimes I'm not, and sometimes I lock myself in the office and curse."
>
> —*Mike, principal*

Teaching isn't an easy job, and we're all doing our best to do the job well. If there is a teacher who pushes your buttons, avoid them. If there is a teacher who inspires you, invite them to lunch. If you are the type of teacher who thinks nothing of asking everyone else for a favor, do your best to understand that your personal mission might not be a priority. That doesn't make other people bad teachers, it just makes them human.

TEACHABLE TAKEAWAYS

We can learn something from every type of teacher. The popular teachers show us how to perform. The old-school ones show us how to endure. The crafty ones inspire our creativity. The slackers teach us to not work harder, but smarter. They take mental health days often and they're happier, better teachers because of it.

> "Teachers are underappreciated and underpaid even though they are passionate, lifelong learners, and necessary for other professions."
>
> —*Jen, teacher*

The important thing is to let different aspects of our personalities shine at the right time. We should be mindful of what we say, how we say it, and who we are trying to impress. There is a time to be patient and accommodating, and there is a time to be eager and stubborn. We can be outspoken or quiet, and we should choose our behavior based on the circumstances. Our students enjoy the fact that we each have different, unique personalities. Their success depends on our diversity because it helps them connect with us on multiple levels. We are each going to be popular with different types of kids, and that's important. We might not be perfect, but we are our own type of teacher. We should take pride in who we are as individuals while learning from our peers.

Teacher's Classroom Survival Kit

Band-Aids: Especially for when our shoes give us blisters.
Coffee: Lots and lots of coffee.
Nail file: There's nothing worse than a hangnail.
Breath mints: The antidote to all of the coffee.
Snacks: Nobody likes a hangry teacher.
Safety pins: For wardrobe malfunctions.
Essential oils: To battle body odor.
Blanket: When school HVAC systems run amok.
Mini-fridge and microwave: To avoid waiting in lunch lines.
Sense of humor: Otherwise, what are we even doing?

HOW TO PRETEND YOU ARE A MORNING PERSON

This lesson will help tired teachers understand the basic concepts of practicing successful early-morning behaviors, such as brewing delicious coffee, waking up on the right side of the bed, and planning for chaos by developing a positive attitude before leaving the house.

"Being a great teacher is all about building relationships. My team members inspire me to become a better teacher by providing ever-changing ways in which they connect with students and fellow staff members."

—Corrin, teacher

DESCRIPTION

Analyzing and applying early-morning methods of adult human function, such as arriving at work on time, appearing energetic before sunrise, and remembering to wear undergarments.

OCCUPATIONAL AREAS

Childhood education, Coffee making, Personal styling, Drama and theatrics, Home care, Speed racing.

ADULT CONCEPTS

Teachers will understand how to:

- Differentiate between an acceptable amount of snooze time and a sad display of neglect.
- Navigate to the bathroom with one eye open.
- Practice beneficial hygiene techniques like remembering to brush teeth.
- Smooth out wrinkled pants by hanging them near a steaming shower.
- Demonstrate the coordination skills required to shower without getting soap into eyes.
- Experiment with a variety of soaps, lotions, and self-help techniques that may inspire basic motor skills expected of adults who have a job.
- Problem-solve how to pack a lunch in less than thirty seconds.
- Develop a workout routine other than stomping around in search of a matching sock.
- Critically think about how to incorporate expired food or stale bread into a packed lunch.
- Challenge physics by beating expected arrival time without breaking any traffic laws.

LESSON OBJECTIVES

Teachers will be able to:

- Arrive at work early, on time, or before students are waiting at the classroom door.
- Access a professional wardrobe that does not pose a threat for twinning with a student.
- Analyze and outsmart the timing of traffic lights.
- Compare and contrast how to inhale a hot cup of coffee without spilling it everywhere.
- Calculate the exact number of minutes required to rush out the door without waking a spouse who has a job that starts at a normal business hour.
- Research, imagine, and mentally plan daily classroom activities while driving to school.
- Explore the possibility of an earlier bedtime despite the temptation to actually have a life.

SUPPLIES NEEDED

Alarm clock, Slip-on shoes, Toothbrush, Toothpaste, Coffee grinds, Coffee maker, Spill-proof travel coffee mug, Lunch box, Bleeding heart, Under-eye concealer, Paper bag to put over head, Hairbrush, Car keys, Will to survive.

ACTIVITIES

Teachers will:

- Prepare a work wardrobe at the start of the week.
- Brew coffee before speaking out loud to anyone.
- Set multiple alarms on a variety of devices in anticipation of power failure or malfunction.
- Practice positive behaviors such as quietly humming a song while exuberantly opening window shades.
- Turn on all of the lights in the house to simulate sunrise and a hopeful outlook.

- Wake with enough time to explore an optimistic aerobics activity.
- Aspire to eat something other than a stale granola bar for breakfast.
- Construct a meal-prep plan that involves more than old pizza and aluminum foil.
- Apply sunglasses to conceal crow's feet and deter blinding sun glare.
- Practice a convincing tone of happiness by repeating things like, "Beautiful day!" and, "I'm great! How are you?" into the car's rearview mirror while trying not to cry.
- Prepare for the day ahead by taking deep, intentional breaths and remembering, "I can do this," and, "I have good benefits."

EVALUATION

- The school clock
- The morning bell and loudspeaker announcements
- Traffic laws
- Peer judgment
- Student empathy

Top 10 Teacher Movies

Blackboard Jungle (1955)
Up the Down Staircase (1967)
Stand and Deliver (1988)
Dead Poets Society (1989)
Lean on Me (1989)
Kindergarten Cop (1990)
Mr. Holland's Opus (1995)
The Substitute (1995)
School of Rock (2003)
Bad Teacher (2011)

Chapter 2

EDUCATIONAL ESSENTIALS

We teachers are sometimes so busy taking care of other people and their problems during the school day that we neglect to respond to our own physical and mental needs. Our bodies could be screaming for hydration and a bathroom break and we ignore the call. It's only until the chaos calms down by mid-afternoon that we realize we are running on pure passion and determination. Then, hopefully, we find enough time to make it to a toilet before peeing our pants or passing out in public.

Teachers are mystical pros in the classroom, but our magic wands seem to burn out in the school parking lot. We sit and wait like minions while watching thirty school buses depart in front of us. The stop-and-go traffic on the drive home just gives us more time to think about the chores we don't feel like doing when we get there. Our own problems pile up alongside the dishes and the laundry. We can juggle thirty professional tasks at once, but sometimes we fail to keep a personal balance for ourselves. Our minds and bodies might run like machines during the school year, but that means we have to give ourselves the same kind of love and support  when we're off-duty. Otherwise, we too will break down, and it usually happens at the worst possible time. We're teachers, not wizards (although, that would be cool). We have to be sensible!

"I hope my students learn to be good people, and that their mistakes don't define them. I obviously want them to learn about English, but I think it's the life lessons that are essential."

—*Casey, teacher*

SENSE OF TOUCH

As teachers, we learn to read body language and other tangible cues to communicate with our students in ways that encourage them. We also become hyper-aware of our own surroundings and every germy thing we touch. We keep hand sanitizer attached to our hips like cowboys hoisting a pistol. Hand sanitizer, the flu shot, and prayers are our only chance at making it through the winter.

It's believed that our sense of touch is the first one we develop, and we begin to explore this as soon as eight weeks old in our mother's womb. Understanding the power of touch and our longtime connection with it can help us unwind after a long day (or simply get through the day without losing our minds). When we feel like

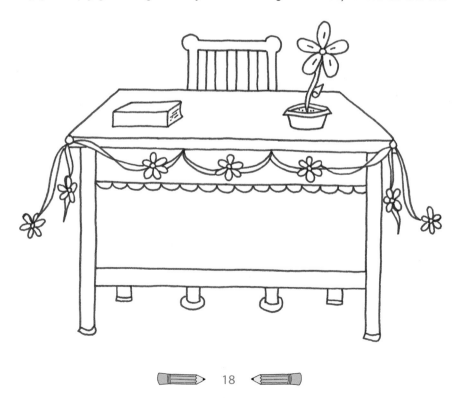

we're going to scream at unruly children, we should squeeze a stress ball instead. The distraction will keep us from saying something we don't mean or spewing out inappropriate language. Alongside our stress balls, we should keep back scratchers and hand lotion in our desk drawers, too. Hand sanitizer might keep germs away but it also sucks us dry.

When you get home from work and feel like punching a wall or passing out, brew yourself a nice bubble bath. The soothing and relaxing bath water will seep into your skin and head straight to the brain to calm you down. Just try not to fall asleep and drown, because you do have another long day of work on par for tomorrow, and your students are counting on you to show up.

> "The most fulfilling aspect of my job is when students come back to chat about what they are doing now. It's amazing how much they remember. It helps remind me why I do the job. Students going off to college telling me that I sparked their interest in science . . . amazing."
>
> —*Corrin, teacher*

SENSE OF SIGHT

We might like students to believe that we have eyes in the back of our heads, but the truth is, some of our eyesight isn't all that perfect. Glasses give some teachers a more studious edge, and peripheral vision is important when walking through a hallway crowded with teenagers who move like zombies. Not to mention, our eyeballs endure a lot throughout the day. We stare at computers and try not to blink when monitoring our classrooms during an observation.

We are always on the lookout for what might go wrong while embracing and encouraging what's been done right. It's a tricky balance, and even though our eyeballs operate like little cameras with a lens, they aren't recording. We experience a lot of learning moments in the classroom. While we may try to remember everything by heart, it's a good idea to keep a journal and document these moments. That's easier said than done, but writing down reflections even once a week can really be beneficial not only to our growth as educators but also in managing our stress at home. Keeping track of moments that make you proud and ones that drive you crazy will give you a good laugh or a good defense. It's a source of

entertainment heading into the summer and a seat belt on the roller-coaster ride you take to get there.

> "The most challenging aspect of teaching is getting all or most of your students to care about their education. We can teach the best lesson in the world, but if the kids don't care, we aren't going to be effective."
>
> *—Casey, teacher*

SENSE OF SOUND

We may often notice that children have selective hearing, especially when we are in the middle of explaining directions. This doesn't necessarily mean their eardrums are broken or their sense of sound is impaired. They might just have trouble paying attention. Sound competes with the other senses. Listening comprehension and the challenges we face with it as teachers can be a frustrating thing to deal with, especially because we don't have time to robotically repeat ourselves over and over again. So, maybe we can't clone ourselves (unless we teach science), but we can use our teacher voices to let others know we're losing patience. Children might not be making deliberate choices about what they hear, but we certainly can. Only you can decide the best way to prepare for the day or unwind on the way home. Books on tape, your favorite musical artist, and talk radio are all good options depending on your mood.

Playing school-appropriate music during class is also a great way to set a particular tone for your instruction and create an inviting learning environment. You can even make an activity out of having students help you make a playlist, though you might regret promising to play their favorite songs.

SENSE OF TASTE

The five sub-tastes that fall under the gustation category include sweet, salty, bitter, sour, and savory. Could this respective progression in descriptive tastes also indicate our evolution through an academic year?

We start out sweet as pie. We have energy, stamina, and motivation. We are bound to succeed on September's sugary high! We can save every child, we

know we can. We're rested. We're ready. We're doing it. Except, sugar highs tend to spike. In a little while, we become salty. We try to pull ourselves back up off the floor but this familiar taste forming has us parched and exhausted. We can't quench our thirst because there isn't time to breathe. School administrators are aware of this phenomenon and so the academic schedule usually gives us a break with a holiday weekend or teacher convention. We get the minimal rest we need to tame our fall season cough, but toughing it out leaves us slightly bitter in spite of the great benefits granting us a low copay. Cozy pajamas are the perfect addition to the bitter pity party we aim to throw ourselves every Friday night. Somehow, we always pull ourselves out of it by Monday morning—even if the coffee tastes just a bit sour.

The second half of the school year leaves us puckering up and sucking it up as we coast on toward savory summer. We celebrate our accomplishments by soaking up sunrays and sipping on adult beverages until the time comes to start the cycle all over again. No wonder we are exhausted!

SENSE OF SMELL

Smell is the most powerful human sense and it can trigger memories of events we can barely recollect otherwise. This is likely not surprising. Every teacher has encountered some kind of pungent smell at some point, and it tends to leave an impression on us. The stench of dodgeball and dirty socks competes with our concentration. We endure this harmless bio warfare to encourage learning. Our best antidote is a cheap air freshener and a stubborn will not to gag. Managing stench that surrounds us during school hours is one thing, but fueling our minds and bodies with pleasant aromas when we are off duty is essential.

Essential oils can be a teacher's best friend, considering the power of the nose and the effect certain aromas have on our stress levels. A new perfume has emerged for teachers on a mission! Essential oil: The quintessential source to keeping our heads on straight.

Top Ten Worst Classroom Smells

Tuna fish
Greek yogurt
That one kid
Spray paint
Feet
Farts
Salad dressing
Vomit
Bad breath
Sweat

AROMATHERAPY

Aromatherapy could very well become a home practice that teachers rely on to maintain sanity and build patience for a lengthy career in the classroom. This holistic-healing therapy pulls its power from natural plant extracts. Essential oils smell lovely and they allegedly work to purify your mind, body, and soul. Much of their reputation comes from personal experience rather than scientific reports, but teachers can use all of the help we can get when it comes to taking it easy.

"Teachers are amazing!"
—Corrin, teacher

ANCIENT OILS

It's natural to assume essential oil practices are meant for yoga studios and new-age living, but they can be enjoyed in the comfort of your home and they have long been an age-old custom. For thousands of years, people have been obsessed with figuring out how to extract the soothing and delicate aroma from aromatic plants. Ancient Egyptians, who used aromatic botanicals such as cinnamon and frankincense to counteract the dead carcass smell of mummies, played a big part in promoting the healing use of plant extracts to other parts of the

world. Ancient Rome followed suit after conquering Egypt in 30 BC, and their well-known bath houses became a breeding ground for battling body odor. Take that, Roman stench! Lavender was a popular smoke screen and remains a fan favorite today.

QUALITY IS ESSENTIAL

The important thing to consider when searching for a distinguished company that dabbles in this aromatic area of expertise is their reputation and their process of extraction. Some processes can taint the purity and quality of the plant oil by introducing harmful or icky chemicals. While we might be inclined to cut budgetary corners in some aspects of our lives, essential oils aren't the products we want to skimp on, especially when exploring them as a way to calm our afternoon nerves.

DILUTING THE OILS

Some oils are more potent than others and require dilution using what's called a carrier oil. Common carrier oils include fragmented coconut oil, olive oil, or vegetable oil. It's always good to test your skin in one small spot if you plan on using an oil topically; you don't want to show up at school looking like you got stung by thirty bees in case you have an allergic reaction. As with everything, it's important to act responsibly and practice caution. If you are just starting out with oils, putting a few drops along with water into a diffuser might be the best way to get your feet wet. Keep in mind essential oils may affect everyone differently. It's also important to note that some oils are not recommended for use by women who are pregnant or nursing.

SMELLING GOOD TAKES SMARTS

Although reputable essential oil companies may claim their products treat or prevent particular ailments, the United States Food and Drug Administration may not be regulating them. That means it's on the consumer to consider their own safety when applying these products to their body in some way, whether that be topically or through inhalation. Ingesting oils is a whole different ball game and rarely recommended unless it specifically states it's safe on the label. Just because

an essential oil smells good, doesn't mean it isn't as strong or serious as other pharmaceuticals. Always read the labels of essential oil products and practice intelligent use. Now that we have all of the disclaimers out of the way, let's dive into how popular oils might allegedly give you a little lift when you need a hug or a bit more energy.

LAVENDER

Lavender is a multipurpose oil that is said to provide a soothing effect in more ways than one. Breathing it in can promote relaxation and subsequently a restful sleep—a teacher's dream! Most of us are either so tired we pass out anywhere we sit down, or we are so stressed we're counting our to-do list instead of sheep at midnight. When the stress of a school day has you feeling like you're about to go off the deep end, spritzing a little lavender around your desk might be your ticket to calming down. Keep it around for summer break too because it's said to soothe sunburns when applied topically.

TEA TREE

Tea tree oil is another year-round go-to oil that is said to be antibacterial, anti-inflammatory, antifungal, and antiviral. Some claim it treats skin problems like eczema, psoriasis, athlete's foot, and acne. It kills bacteria, so adding a drop or two to your deodorant might keep you from being known as the teacher with the pit stains. Supposedly, it could also be your first line of defense against nasty head lice invading your scalp.

PEPPERMINT

It's tough to make time for ourselves during the school year, and the go-go-go lifestyle can take its toll on our digestive tracts. Peppermint oil is said to aid in digestion and relax the muscles of the GI tract. Some say it can boost energy and memory, too. Plus, its cooling property can ease a headache, hot flash, or achy muscle. It might be good to keep peppermint around during final exams, or really, any day of the week.

EUCALYPTUS

Eucalyptus allegedly meets mucous membranes on the battlefield of your nostrils. It's said to combat congestion and sooth headaches. So, if you don't enjoy being bogged down by cold medicines for the long months of winter, inhaling some eucalyptus steam might help you breathe easier. Take that, germy children!

ROSEMARY

We've all had those days where we get to school and just can't focus on a thing. Our minds are fret with the thirty things we have to accomplish, and our overwhelming inability to concentrate leads us to become totally unproductive instead. Rosemary is said to boost brain power and improve concentration by promoting clear thinking. It's also said to combat fatigue by jiving up energy. Perhaps taking a whiff of rosemary can be enough to help us make it through an afternoon of proctoring exams.

CINNAMON

Cinnamon is said to promote focus, aid in concentration, and lower frustration levels. Managing our own frustrations is part of the job, but it'd be nice to have a little help from a sweet scent like cinnamon. Don't let the sweetness of cinnamon fool you. This oil is incredibly strong and shouldn't be applied directly to the skin. It should always be diluted. Potent oils like cinnamon require dilution in the same way our truest inner thoughts must be watered down into nicer vocabulary that won't get us into trouble.

LEMON

Lemon is more than just a slice of garnish on our water glass. It's said to ease anxiety and improve mood. Its scent is refreshing and there's a reason it reminds us of a clean home. Lemon is a disinfectant that fights grease, cleans countertops, and polishes wood. Lemon oil can be combined with eucalyptus and peppermint to create a bug spray dream team. Keep it around come summertime.

FRANKINCENSE

Frankincense oil has long been associated with the spiritual realm. So when the reality of the school year has your blood pressure boiling, try adding a few drops of frankincense to a diffuser and meditating on your life choices. This slow breathing exercise may help your spiritual growth while fighting respiratory ailments like asthma, pneumonia, or bronchitis. Frankincense can supposedly also help decrease the appearance of fine lines and wrinkles. With all of those early-morning wakeups, our facial moisturizers can probably use all of the help they can get. What's more, this spellbinding oil can boost the immune system, relieve skin irritations, and allegedly deter flatulence. Less farts in the classroom? Where do we sign up?!

OREGANO

It turns out oregano is more than just a pizza enhancement. It's like a student who has a ton of potential and grows up to actually put all of that talent to good use. This powerhouse oil is a natural antibiotic said to trump bacteria and infections, relieve pain, and reduce inflammation. It can combat common cold symptoms we so frequently encounter as teachers and apparently ease a sore throat, too.

ORANGE

Orange oil can be a game changer when a bad mood has a teacher treading on the crossover between human and supernatural banshee. Spritz some of that citrus around your soul and give your brain new perspective on whether or not you actually want to quit your job or jump off a cliff. Used topically, orange oil can bring new radiance to your skin. If we can't see the sun through the winter months, it would be nice to have some kind of glow, right?

CREATIVE COPING MECHANISMS

It's possible the effects of essential oils are all mental because they smell nice and companies apply good marketing skills to convince us we need them. But it's also possible these powerful oils are legit, and they can play a part in our body's physical response to a chaotic teaching schedule. With all of the creative challenges we face in the classroom, we may as well be inventive about how we cope with them at home. Maybe our heart rate and blood pressure could actually benefit from a simple spray of orange or rub of lavender. We don't really have anything to lose apart from the classroom stench that seeps its way into the stitches of our sweaters. At the very least, we can counteract the smell of sweaty gym bags and body odor!

Chapter 3

NAMASTE A TEACHER

It's only natural for teachers to wonder what life would be like for them in a different career. Would it be easier? Would it be less stressful? Maybe. But it would also likely be less rewarding and not as fulfilling. It's cool that we get to be creative in our work, witness the direct impact of our efforts, and make positive changes. In lieu of a cubicle, we have a classroom. That gives our happy, overworked brains enough space to work things out. Sometimes, we are spending more time with children than with coworkers our own age. A professional day surrounded by adults feels like a breeze compared to the typical chaos of interacting with a new generation of thinkers. It's fine to have fleeting thoughts about the road not taken, but don't think on it too hard. Every job has its challenges, but not every job has the kind of perks we have as teachers. So, when times get tough, get out of your own head and decide that you're not going to call it quits on this incredible opportunity you have to be a teacher. Thinking about making a move? Nah. Not you. You're a teacher for life.

FINDING A BALANCE

Rather than getting frustrated by all of the little things that go into being a teacher, focus on the big stuff you love. Make a list of what keeps you motivated. Don't run away, stay put and breathe. There are times when it's going to be difficult. Stick it out. It's no stretch to compare classroom challenges to the difficulty we feel when holding a pose on a yoga mat. Adopting a regular yoga practice may help you find peace and gratitude in the everyday elements of your work. Plus, you can practice yoga in between classes, on your lunch break, and during your prep period.

BREATHE THROUGH IT

You don't have to be sitting in a trendy yoga studio to practice the foundation of a yoga practice. Yoga breathing, also known as pranayama, can help you relax when you are worried or stressed. When students frustrate you, don't let it ruin your entire day. Instead, take a moment to breathe. Count your inhales and exhales, and perform breath repetitions slowly and evenly. Breathe through your nose if you can, and imagine the tide of the ocean coming in and out like a promise that everything will be okay. The sun will still shine on you in spite of you losing your temper earlier that morning. Even one deep breath has the power to change your outlook. It's helpful, too, to envision something positive. Choose any mantra you like. Breathe in faith; breathe out fear. Breathe in acceptance; breathe out the urge to judge every child who 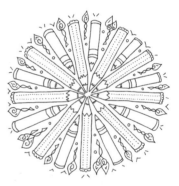 picks his nose in your presence. Breathe in patience; breathe out the desire to scream like a psychopath who forgot to take her meds. You know, it's all about making it your own personal journey.

CHAKRAS

Chakras are personal pathways of energy and our own ties to the universe (if you believe in that sort of thing). Apparently, when energy becomes blocked in a particular chakra, it's bad news. Blockage isn't really good for anybody as it can cause our physical bodies, minds, and souls to become all out of whack. These unnatural buildups of yucky stuff are bound to lead to tendencies of tiredness, anxiousness, and even tummy problems. All seven chakras hold the kind of powers teachers need to succeed.

CROWN CHAKRA

The crown chakra, or "Sahasrara" in Sanskrit, is located at the top of our head and it symbolizes what we know. It's linked to spirituality and enlightenment, a soulful connection with the world around us. As teachers, even if we have the knowledge, we know that we must find a way to connect with students in ways they can relate to or understand. A blocked crown chakra can be a literal headache. If it feels like you can't put one foot in front of the other, you're totally tired all of the time, or you have zero inspiration to do anything at all, your sahasrara might need some loving. Try meditating, sipping on herbal tea, or saying something positive to yourself every morning in the mirror to snap out of it.

THIRD EYE CHAKRA

The third eye chakra, or "Ajna" in Sanskrit, is symbolic of what we see. No, not through our eyeballs, but through our third eye. Didn't know we had one? Well, we do, and it's linked to our imagination and intuition. When our third eye chakra is in good shape, we see things crystal clear. If you happen to run into someone who seems close-minded with little to no self-awareness, give them a break. It could be that their third eye chakra is imbalanced. As teachers, it's obviously important for us to be able to see situations from a variety of viewpoints, and sometimes, we have to accept (or at least do our best to understand) things we might otherwise see differently.

THROAT CHAKRA

The throat chakra, or "Vishuddha" in Sanskrit, is tied to communication, self-expression, and personal integrity. It's a reminder for us to speak our minds

honestly and live out our own personal truths. Unfortunately, this doesn't give teachers a green light to say whatever is on our minds at all times (even though that would be amazing). Speaking our truth doesn't excuse rude remarks, but it does give us permission to say no at times. It also encourages us to politely speak our mind when it's time to be honest with a parent or a student. Anytime you walk out of a difficult parent-teacher conference, know that you did your throat chakra a lot of good. However, if you have a tendency to talk over others during conversation or lack the desire to hear out their side of the story, your throat chakra might need a little toning down!

HEART CHAKRA

Most teachers should be pretty good at keeping their heart chakras in check. After all, the heart chakra, or "Anahata" in Sanskrit, is tied to compassion and healing. Except, we are human, and it's only natural for us to be imperfect. We definitely need to have compassion in the classroom in order to gain the trust and respect of our students. That doesn't mean it's easy to push aside negative feelings when they arise. Your heart chakra might be imbalanced if you find it difficult to forgive others and let things go. If your chest is often heavy or something is weighing on your ability to move forward, do your best to make small changes. Try to see the humor in things, give and receive hugs, and do something nice for someone else. If a student really ticked you off, instead of holding it against them for the rest of the year, give them a fresh start the next day in class. It will be healthy for both of you.

"I hope my students learn to be decent humans who never give up."
—*Nicole, teacher*

SOLAR PLEXUS CHAKRA

The solar plexus chakra, or "Manipura" in Sanskrit, is connected to purpose, self-esteem, and wisdom. It's where we channel our willpower from, and it's where we get our sense of self. As teachers, we need to find a balance in this area. Managing low self-esteem or a huge ego while leading a classroom of children is only going to make our jobs more difficult. We'd either be going home in tears

ourselves, or sending children home crying after harshly schooling them to prove our intelligence! Confidence is important, but so is our delivery. We have to be willing to take creative risks and pursue them, understanding that sometimes things might not work out as planned.

SACRAL CHAKRA

The sacral chakra, or "Svadhisthana" in Sanskrit, represents creativity, sexuality, and emotional balance. If your sacral chakra is in good standing, you're probably a highly passionate person who has no qualms about enjoying healthy pleasures. If it's misaligned, though, you might find yourself taming issues of addiction. If you're a total Type A teacher who has trouble going with the flow every once in a while, think about how important it is to be able to let students lead their own learning at times in the classroom. It might be frustrating to let students find their own way without immediately correcting them, but it will be good for their growth, and for yours.

ROOT CHAKRA

The root chakra, or "Muladhara" in Sanskrit, represents the basic elements that ground your life and keep you stable. It also symbolizes the stuff you need to survive and feel secure. Signs of an imbalanced root chakra manifest themselves in a variety of ways. Are you frightened of losing control over your classroom? Do you think you need to do everything yourself to ensure the job is done the right way? If you'd like to practice some root chakra healing, the next time you are preparing for a substitute teacher to watch over your class in your absence, do your best not to think about how they are doing when you are away. Don't obsess over everything being perfect. Instead, take care of yourself on your day off and trust that things will be fine when you return.

> "My students inspire me to be a better teacher. When I reach them in a lesson and see them engaged, it makes me want to find more ways that will keep them interested and motivated."
>
> —*Kristen, teacher*

FINDING INSPIRATION THROUGH YOGA PRACTICE

Before signing up for a new practice, it's important to talk with your doctor or physician. Yoga teaches us to be mindful and listen to our bodies, to not overstretch or push ourselves too hard. As teachers, it's a breath of fresh air to find a practice that actually encourages us to slow down. The great thing about yoga is that it's not just about building a healthy outside physique. In truth, it's about working on what lies within. It's an activity that breathes comfort into our bodies because it helps us connect all of the things that make us whole. Whether that means through our breath, mind, or soul, the movement and positions encourage us to find a balance. We either breathe through transitions or learn to hold a pose through its discomfort. As human beings and as teachers, we require the energy, mindset, and belief that we can withstand change or hold our ground. Yoga is all about balance, and every teacher knows how important it is for us to maintain a happy medium in our careers. Even more so, finding a balance in all aspects of our lives makes us happier people, which in turn makes us better teachers.

Best Yoga Poses for Teachers
Mountain Pose: It gives us good posture.
Downward Facing Dog: It's fun and feels amazing.
Cat-Cow: For all of those neck and shoulder knots.
Chair Pose: Because we are strong.
Warriors 1, 2 & 3: Hello? We're warriors on a mission.
Triangle Pose: It lengthens our waist and stretches our legs.
Tree Pose: It teaches us balance and faith.
Bridge Pose: Because we are the bridge between today and tomorrow.
Child's Pose: Because sometimes we give up.
Legs up the Wall: Because our feet deserve a break.
Corpse Pose: Because sometimes we are dead.

HOW TO BE A GOOD YOGI

This lesson will provide teachers with a flexible and lighthearted approach to handling all sorts of annoyances while encouraging them to play on mats like carefree children.

DESCRIPTION

Transferring a mindful yoga practice over to life in and outside of the classroom by connecting the mind, body, and spirit through playful movement, sweet arm balances, and a happy attitude.

OCCUPATIONAL AREAS

Soul searching, Stretching, Personal hygiene, Relaxation, Breathing, Sleeping, Meditating, Chanting, Holistic health, Sanskrit.

ADULT CONCEPTS

Teachers will understand how to:

- Attend a laid-back yoga studio that is chill, inviting, and plays good music.
- Avoid pretentious yoga studios that judge workout apparel and lifestyle habits.
- See beauty in common activities like silently staring into space or chanting gibberish.
- Develop a proactive mind-over-body belief system, especially when writing lesson plans.
- Let go of neuroses such as worrying about how many calories are in a doughnut.
- Demonstrate the mindful ability to avert or embrace flatulence during a one-hour class.
- Problem-solve how to bend in ways that don't seem human.
- Choose positive affirmations such as gratitude over adverse thoughts like jealousy.
- Realize acceptance is necessary for leading the good life.

 35

LESSON OBJECTIVES

Teachers will be able to:

- Be a warrior, not a worrier.
- Be flexible in all aspects of life, except when it's time to put their foot down.
- Balance on one leg while comparing tree pose to calmly multitasking like a boss.
- Push their bodies when the challenge is manageable and the mind is strong.
- Differentiate between using child's pose to relax and the fetal position to cry like a baby.
- Expunge negative thoughts through deep breathing techniques.
- Let things go without letting everything go to hell.
- Breath audibly to lower blood pressure and send a message to unruly students.
- Develop personal mantras that apply to the classroom such as, "I will not lose my mind today," and "I will remain as stable as a tree in a hurricane of chaotic children."
- Eat a third slice of pizza without guilt—the body wants what the body wants.
- Avoid germs and hover over toilet seats by practicing chair pose in bathroom stalls.

SUPPLIES NEEDED

Yoga mat, Yoga block, Yoga strap, Leggings, Scrunchie, Reggae music, Candles, Hippie beads, Posters with happy quotes, Buddha statue, Goats and/or puppies.

ACTIVITIES

Teachers will:

- Avoid comparing themselves to others or dwelling on things they cannot control.
- Embrace the opportunity to live in the moment with each inhale.

- Breathe power, confidence, and strength into each pose.
- Practice yoga poses between classes to maintain a chill vibe.
- Release negative thoughts and worries with each exhale.
- Listen to their bodies when they want to pass out on a yoga mat.
- Meditate on positive thoughts such as gratitude and patience.
- Try not to think about cake during savasana.
- Practice backbends that feel good while resisting the urge to bend over backwards for everyone at all times.
- Bring a towel to class to avoid dripping sweat all over someone else's mat.
- Practice yoga handstands at home against a wall to feel young and free.

EVALUATION

- Absolutely nothing other than personal satisfaction

Top Ten School-Related TV Shows

Saved by the Bell
Hangin' with Mr. Cooper
Freaks and Geeks
Welcome Back, Kotter
Vice Principals
Head of the Class
Fame
Our Miss Brooks
Boy Meets World
Teachers

Chapter 4

AFTER-SCHOOL
HAPPY HOURS

Before you can become a better teacher, you have to be a better you. That means taking care of yourself and making time for your own personal endeavors and needs. We're often cramming so much into our brains that our bodies feel sluggish. It's easy to get caught up in the hustle and bustle of everyday, and it's even easier to make excuses not to exercise after running around in every other way.

Being active and fit isn't only about maintaining a healthy physique, it's about being happy. Scientific studies have drawn a link between happiness and exercise, though it isn't clear if one causes the other to happen or if the two are just soulmates who appear together often. People tend to feel better and have a brighter outlook when they move around. Think about those sporty teacher types. Are they ever really in a bad mood? If they are, they likely burn it out of their system  by running on the track or climbing a rock wall. Think about hyper-energetic dogs who just want to play. Once they get their exercise, they're satisfied and well-behaved. The same is true for children, and for us. Play is necessary.

ACTIVELY PURSUING HAPPINESS

There's a reason our brains work better after we've performed some type of physical activity. Feeling stressed, overwhelmed, and worried is typical for any adult. The happier ones tend to have some type of outlet to release all of that junk, like wringing out a soggy dish towel that's holding on to heavy water weighing it down. We too can sometimes use a rinse through the washing machine. The twisting, turning, and flipping around can be good for us. We need to work out the kinks in our system and come out of the dryer feeling fluffy, soft, and brand new. As teachers, we feel ourselves managing a fight-or-flight response to lots of stuff we deal with on a daily basis. Sometimes, we just want to run out the back door and straight to our cars, fleeing from every responsibility and heading straight for our beds. Other times, we fight the urge to fight our students on little issues that get under our skin.

Our brains perceive exercise as a threat and a different form of stress that they're not used to managing. Our hearts start pumping, our sweat glands are cued up, and we naturally enter another moment of choice: fight or flight? In order to maintain composure, our brains release a protein called BDNF, or brain-derived neurotrophic factor. This protein is like an adorable little protective bubble for our bodies. It's meant to comfort us and help us relax. Essentially, it's the subconscious button our brains have on speed dial so that it doesn't feel like everything else is pushing our buttons in a bad way. That's why exercise makes us feel so good. It clears our heads and we have a fresh start.

BUILT TO BE GOOD

Luckily for us, our bodies are literally built to combat stress, if we put them to good use. When we exercise, we release endorphins. Endorphins are hormones that serve as a catalyst for a happy mood. They block pain and other discomfort by creating a sense of euphoria, reminding us that life is good. Maybe some of our professional development days should involve some kind of workout so that we can invite endorphins along for the ride!

After all, getting in a good workout not only helps us sleep, it makes us look and feel good. Actually, it makes us feel good for a long time, as regular exercise can help lower our risk for all kinds of yucky diseases and health problems. Active

and fit humans are less likely to develop heart disease, stroke, diabetes, and even several types of cancer. It keeps our bones strong and our joints in good shape. It can even help shape our minds in a way that protects memory and thinking skills. Depending on what you enjoy doing, there are plenty of options for teachers who want to become more active. You just have to find what's right for you and your personality.

RUNNING

Running is an activity that makes you feel strong and weak at the same time. It's not just a workout for your legs and your lungs, but your mind, too. It teaches patience, endurance, and dedication. It gives you the confidence that you can overcome any mountain in your way. The important thing to remember when building a running routine is that every single person runs at their own pace. It's great to be competitive, but not necessarily with others. Be competitive with yourself, instead. Push your own limits. It's a personal journey and a race against yourself, even when you join a running club or find a running buddy.

If you find it difficult to get started, begin with a walk/run routine. The increments can be as small as you like, and it can be as simple as marking a route around your neighborhood. Run to one light post or mailbox, then walk the next two blocks. Create your own path. Set little goals for yourself, and eventually, you may want to strive for more. No matter the distance or how you get there, it's an accomplishment. Just like there's nothing like reaching the end of the school year, there's no better feeling than finishing a race.

WALKING

Walking offers up a lot of the same benefits as running, and it's less harsh on your joints. A brisk walk can clear your head and bring you joy. It's a great low-impact alternative to running. The best part is you can do this anytime, anywhere, and you don't necessarily need to be sporting workout clothes to get it done. All you need is a comfortable pair of shoes and you're off!

If your mind is racing during your prep period or you're stuffed from lunch, think about taking a stroll through the hallway or around the outdoor track. All you need is ten to twenty minutes to get some fresh air and get moving. Some of the best creative ideas flow to your brain during a good workout. Going for a walk

while bringing your phone is also a great way to catch up with a family member or old friend while burning some calories.

HIKING

Speaking of getting outdoors, when the weather cooperates, hiking is a fabulous option for feeling good. In fact, studies show that simply spending time outside can offer benefits similar to exercise. We spend too many hours in front of computer screens, televisions, and phones. We aren't robots—we're human! Our brains aren't built for remembering thirty different password combinations. It's no wonder we feel like our heads are going to explode at times. If we take the conscious time to step away from all of this, resetting ourselves can be as simple as resetting one of those annoying passwords. Simply being outside in a green space can be enough to reboot ourselves, but most of us do not see the light of day enough, especially during the winter months. Make it a priority to get outside, whether that means going to a park, a hiking trail, or simply a courtyard.

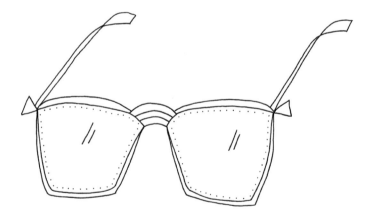

BOXING

Like yoga, boxing can help us cope with our problems by giving us an outlet that encourages us to breathe through movement. Sometimes, we need something a little stronger than downward dog to keep our bad energy at bay. The challenges of

any career might send us home feeling like we need to throw a jab at something. So, grab yourself a heavy bag or a boxing gym membership and throw down your frustrations in a healthy way that breaks a sweat.

Boxers are arguably in the best physical shape of any competitive athlete. It's not just the jabs, hooks, and uppercuts getting them ripped. Their workouts are difficult, enjoyable, and they inspire a youthful spirit. They might leave you wondering how you were able to jump rope so easily back in the good old days, but you'll be happy to be back at it again.

OLD-SCHOOL FITNESS

Speaking of being a kid again, a great option for adult exercise is to rekindle our love for things we enjoyed doing as children. If your favorite childhood memories were spent on a field somewhere, maybe it's time to relive your glory days. Most communities offer social team sports like softball, volleyball, and soccer.

Working out doesn't have to feel like a chore, but it should be done safely. Yes, we may have thought helmets and kneepads were nerdy when we were young, dumb, and able to bounce back. Today, falls take their toll on our tailbones and our egos. So, strap on the safety accessories before hopping on a skateboard or into an old pair of rollerblades. It will be a fun workout, but give yourself a break on the speed and try not to break any bones when you cruise downhill!

SWIMMING

Swimming is an ideal cardiovascular workout for anyone looking for a low-impact alternative. It's a perfect option for all ages as it is considered both a cardio and strength training workout. As we get older, high-impact workouts are more difficult to maintain. Swimming builds stamina, cardiovascular strength, and muscle strength. It teaches you to breathe mindfully. Not to mention, swimming regularly may not only delay the effects of aging, it can deter all of the inconvenient health problems that come with aging. Exercising while being submerged under water helps your mind and body relax and chill out. It also helps us feel that much closer to summer.

BIKING

Riding a bike is another low-impact option for those of us looking to get our heart rates up without breaking our knees in the process. There are many different levels of biking, too. You can be intense about your ride, whether you're on the road, in the mountains, or at a spin class. You can also decide that you just feel like cruising around the neighborhood. You might not burn the same amount of calories, but feeling the breeze on your face while you put your arms out to a T will definitely give you new perspective on your day. It's just like being a neighborhood kid again; no cell phones, no checking in, just be home by the time dinner is on the table.

COUNTRY CLUBBING

Feeling snazzy? Maybe it's time to trade in the teaching loafers for tennis shoes. Tennis, golf, and badminton are all calling your name down at the local country club. Spending a day out on the green might not be quite as taxing as putting in a twenty-minute cardio session, but it will do wonders for your heart. There's

something about the science of golf that calms the mind. Sure, it can be frustrating, but it's also an awesome opportunity to spend the day with friends.

HOME PROJECTS

Is there a project at home that's been on your to-do list? Sometimes, if our minds are preoccupied with too many thoughts, it helps to physically organize something, like our closet, or put our hands to good use. Working on the car in the garage, tidying up the yard by sweeping up leaves, mowing the lawn, and even gardening are all simple ways for us to feel accomplished while burning calories. Plus, we have the added benefit of bragging to our spouses about how much we did that day to make our home lives better.

LEADING A HEALTHY LIFESTYLE

Okay, so there's nothing wrong with us driving to the gym and looking for the parking spot nearest to the door. Hey, we don't want to have to walk that far on the way to our "real" workout. Except, if you're the type of person who doesn't have the time to carve a "real" workout into your day, there's plenty of ways to get some exercise without even having to think about it.

> "I hope my students learn how to think for themselves and use their skills to figure things out and solve problems, big or small. I also hope they learn that everyone has something to offer."
>
> —Jen, teacher

Park far and walk the distance. Take the stairs. Do the laundry. Dance around the kitchen. Dust your house. Do something that gets you up off the couch or away from your desk. It's mentally beneficial to stay busy. Yes, all people can benefit from exercise, but teachers especially. Knowing all of the benefits still doesn't make it easy to carve these healthy activities into our daily lives.

Many people make excuses about not having the time or the money to make small changes in their daily routine. Teachers do start their days earlier than most, and we do have a lot on our plates. But there are ways to integrate exercise into the work week. You don't have to subscribe to an expensive gym to make a commitment. Make a promise to yourself, and take some of your own advice. We so often lecture school children about their need to become responsible, committed, and dedicated to the work they do in our classes. We've heard every single excuse in the book about why they didn't do their homework or study for a test. Making excuses is part of human nature, and life is full of excuses. Stop letting excuses get in the way of your own personal happiness. If you don't have the time, make time. If you don't have the money, get outside—the outdoors are free! If you don't have the energy, do your best to get through the first week of working out and you'll have more energy. Find something you enjoy doing, and give yourself permission to put other commitments on hold so that you can keep a promise to yourself. Happiness is attainable, and it's a choice. Choose to be happy, and get a head start on your summer beach bod before it's too late.

Top Ten School Movies

Grease (1978)
Fast Times at Ridgemont High (1982)
The Breakfast Club (1985)
Back to School (1986)
Ferris Bueller's Day Off (1986)
School Ties (1992)
Billy Madison (1995)
Election (1999)
October Sky (1999)
Mean Girls (2004)

Chapter 5

THE GOOD STUFF

It's important to take time out of the day to happily treat ourselves. For some of us, a "happy hour" equates to simply having a moment to ourselves. No questions. No noise. No chaos. Add to that the sweet or sour bliss of a comforting spirit, and we can collect our thoughts in peace or dance them away without a care in the world.

Not every adult establishment and watering hole is going to agree on a set time for happy hour, but the smart ones will start at 3:00 p.m., just about when the afternoon school bell rings and teachers are ready to flood their bellies with the good stuff. Okay, flood is a strong word. Sophisticated teachers sip their drinks. We don't slurp, and we try not to slur our language either. Stressed teachers are an exception; we fight the urge to slug back cocktails like we just crossed the Sahara and booze is our only hydration source. *Kidding!* We are responsible adults. No judgment here though if you do slug like a sailor, so long as you are safe, mindful, and reasonable about where, when, and how much you consume. By the time Friday afternoon rolls around, some of us do feel like we've taken a trip through the desert. Our lips are chapped. Our work clothes have stains on them, and we're thirsty. The only difference is that our skin is pale and pasty. What happened to that summer tan, anyway? Maybe it's hiding somewhere under the bar in Margaritaville.

ALL IN GOOD FUN

Obviously, alcohol consumption is no solution to the weight we carry home on our shoulders. A good beer is not going to solve our problems or write our lesson plans, but there's a difference between chilling back with a nice cocktail and sucking down so many of them we flush out our brain cells. Still, just because teachers are leaders of children during the work week does not mean we can't responsibly blow off some steam when we get home. Of course, it's important that we keep a level head in spite of lowering our inhibitions.

"The most fulfilling aspect of my job is when the student who has really been struggling finally 'gets it' or has, as we say in education, 'the light bulb moment.' It's also when former students keep in touch and you hear of their successes and the impact that you made on them."

—Jen, teacher

Clearly all in good fun; beer, wine, and spirits are obviously not a solution to true anxiety. We're teachers. We've seen the horror stories and the video tutorials about alcohol abuse. Consuming any form of alcohol in unhealthy amounts is sure to bring on more stress, more problems, and more belly weight. Plus, most grownups find it hard to get up in the morning, period. Adding a few glasses of wine to that equation makes dragging ourselves out the door on Monday morning that much more difficult.

Every teacher knows that the academic year gives us plenty of reasons and opportunities to celebrate and treat ourselves. We don't have the luxury of taking a vacation every time we need a break; we're at the mercy of the school schedule. Pairing cocktails with particular teaching moments and celebrations can give us a glimpse at what happy hour might feel like on a beach somewhere. Sometimes, small treats that help us relax are the perfect ticket to staying strong, fueled, and in control after a long day's work.

BACK-TO-SCHOOL NIGHT

Back-to-school night marks the start of a new school year when teachers are well-rested and ready to take on anything. We have all of the energy in the world to display our amazing and entertaining personalities on a silver platter. Hosting back-to-school night is like going to a job fair where you are trying to impress literally every person you encounter. Sure, it's fun and informative, but it can also feel hectic, exciting, and exhausting! We want to make a great impression. By the end of the night, our faces are numb from all of the smiling and talking about our subject knowledge. We could really use a sophisticated cocktail to liven up our spirits.

A dirty vodka martini is the perfect choice for this pairing. Why? Because most back-to-school nights are smooth and sloppy at the same time. Our charm and charisma masks the nerves hiding in our sweaty shoes. Be sure to lift one pinky

up while you sip on this bad boy at the staff after-party and you'll be the coolest kid in the room.

Speaking of cool, a perfect non-alcoholic alternative for back-to-school night is cucumber-infused water. Talking all night can leave a teacher parched and tired, and at that point there's nothing better than a crisp, hydrating glass of the good stuff.

How to Make a Dirty Vodka Martini

Ice
½ ounce dry vermouth
3 ounces vodka
½ ounce olive juice
Toothpick, for serving

Fill a shaker with ice. Pour in the dry vermouth. Shake! Dump the ice. Put new ice in the used shaker, pouring in the vodka and olive juice. Stir! Stab some olives with a toothpick. Strain the concoction into a martini glass, garnishing with olives. Bartending tip: Don't worry so much about measuring every ingredient perfectly. You can add more or less olive juice and dry vermouth to suit your own personal tastes.

PARENT-TEACHER CONFERENCES

If back-to-school night is a job fair, parent-teacher conferences are the second interview. It's an up-close and personal time when teachers and parents have the chance to sit down and get to know one another better. It gives teachers great perspective on students, and it gives parents a window into what their children are doing all day in school. Obviously, parents want to hear good things about their kids. This is a great time for us to gush about the students who are shining stars and calmly describe why students may be struggling. Sometimes, we have to be honest while not being offensive or disrespectful. There is a certain type of finesse required when having a tough conversation with a parent.

That's why the after-party drink for parent-teacher conferences has to be a classic whiskey sour. The bourbon, whiskey, or scotch base gives it a nice kick, just like the backbone we need to have those tough, sugar-coated talks. Don't forget the cherry on top! (It falls to the bottom, but that's beside the point). If bourbon isn't your cup of tea and you're looking for something kid-friendly, treat yourself to a root beer float. The foamy and frothy cup of something frosty is bound to help chill you out.

How to Make a Whiskey Sour

Ice
1½ ounce whiskey, bourbon, or scotch
½ ounce simple syrup
1 ounce lemon juice
Cherry, for serving

Fill a cocktail shaker with ice. Pour in all of the ingredients. Shake it up while dancing around your kitchen. Strain into a glass. Add some of the ice cubes and a cherry. Bartending tip: Combine a shot of whiskey with store-bought sour mix, shake it up, and you're good to go.

EEK! GRADES ARE DUE!

No matter what, grade deadlines have a habit of sneaking up on us. It doesn't matter how well we plan. Our rubrics might be organized and perfectly explained. Our assessments might be reasonable and fair. We could be the best teacher on the face of the Earth, and still, the week that grades are due, we're running around like chickens with their heads cut off.

Instead of banging your head against the wall when a student asks to submit work at the last minute, go home and treat yourself to a Harvey Wallbanger. If your cold, sober heart just dished out a bunch of bad grades and you feel like warming up, shoot for a lovely spot of caffeine-free herbal tea instead. You don't have to worry about staying awake any longer. Time to go to bed!

How to Make a Harvey Wallbanger

Ice
1½ ounce vodka
4 ounces orange juice
½ ounce Galliano
Orange slice, for serving
Cherry, for serving

Fill a highball glass with ice. Pour in vodka and orange juice. Stir! Float some Galliano on top. Garnish with a slice of orange and a cherry. Bartending tip: You can also just pour in the Galliano—it's all going to the same place anyway.

OBSERVATION: DID FAB!

There's nothing like having an administrator walk into your classroom on a perfect day when every student is invested, intrigued, and engaged in their creative work. Ah—this is the classroom you imagined building when you signed up to be a teacher. This is the jackpot of all great lesson plans! It's hard to describe this kind of happy place because it might be different for every teacher. Whatever it means for you, the sense of satisfaction, accomplishment, and merit felt when your hard work pays off is pure joy. It's like heaven is spritzing your face with the fountain of youth and a touch of glitter.

Earning a good observation rating is something to be proud of because you're a pro and you deserve a pat on the back. So, bask in the glory of paradise and fix yourself a cocktail with the same name. Need something a little less strong? Pick up a bottle of sparkling apple cider instead. Pour it into a flute glass because you're fancy like that.

How to Make a Paradise

1½ ounce gin
1 ounce apricot brandy
2 ounces orange juice
Ice

Pour gin, apricot brandy, and orange juice into a cocktail shaker
filled with ice. Shake! Strain into a fancy glass and add ice if you like.
Bartending tip: Drink umbrella, sunglasses, and shoes optional.

OBSERVATION: GONE BAD!

Being observed is part of a teacher's rite of annual passage. It's an opportunity for higher-ups to give us a high-five or a finger pointing. Sure, we all want to do a good job every day we show up to work, but that's just not how the real world works. We might be tired, sick, or flustered. We cannot always be on our A game. There's no bigger letdown than having your bad day show up on a piece of paper meant to measure your teaching ability.

Don't worry, grasshopper, there is always something new to learn. Don't get too down on yourself if you don't earn a glowing score every time you are observed. Use the feedback as constructive criticism and do your best to be better next time. Instead of carrying the weight of the bad grade on your back, wash it down with the right beverage pairing: A Grasshopper. If you are craving a sweet treat to help you cope, spoon up a bowl of chocolate mint-chip ice cream instead.

How to Make a Grasshopper

Ice
1 ounce crème de menthe
1 ounce crème de cacao
1 ounce half-and-half or heavy cream

Fill a cocktail shaker with ice. Add all ingredients. Shake! Strain into a chilled martini glass. Bartending tip: Sprinkle chocolate sauce around the interior of a chilled martini glass prior to pouring ingredients.

PROCTORING EXAMS

It's no mystery that most kids today would rather be doing anything other than taking a standardized test, midterm, or final exam. They are in good company because most teachers would prefer to be doing anything other than proctoring. There's a sense of camaraderie among colleagues because everyone knows it bites the dust, but we do it with a smile because it's part of the job.

Okay, okay. Tests are important. They're required and our presence is necessary. But most teachers love teaching because we can talk, interact, and communicate with kids. Quiet time would be great if we were able to perform other tasks while students were kept busy, but that's not how proctoring works. It doesn't matter if we are pros at multitasking. When we proctor exams, we have to be stern, strict, and hyper-focused.

That's why proctoring is like stepping on a rusty nail. We feel like we need shots afterward, but instead of getting sloppy, we can sip on a stiff drink later that evening. If drinks aren't your thing, treat yourself to an after-school pedicure. Standing in a silent room for hours takes a toll on your poor little feet.

How to Make a Rusty Nail

Ice
1½ ounce scotch whiskey
¾ ounce Drambuie

Fill a rocks glass with ice. Add all ingredients. Stir! Bartending tip: Garnish with a lemon twist.

ANY GIVEN WEEKNIGHT

By no means is this an endorsement for teachers to throw back drinks every other night of the week, but every hard-working professional knows we don't always need an excuse to enjoy a delicious cocktail. The career of a teacher is an emotional roller-coaster, and there's creative drink pairings for every feeling out there.

WHEN YOU FEEL OLD

Did you make a pop-culture reference that completely went over your students' heads? Did they make you feel ancient and wise beyond your years? When you've had that kind of day, you might think about fixing yourself up a nice old-fashioned while reminiscing about the good old days with a friend, colleague, or partner at home. Non-alcoholic alternative: Cream Soda or Birch Beer.

How to Make an Old-Fashioned

Orange slice
Cocktail cherry
2 dashes angostura bitters
1 sugar cube
Splash of water
Ice
1½ ounce bourbon or rye whiskey

Place an orange slice and cocktail cherry at the bottom of a rocks glass. Add bitters, sugar, and a splash of water. Muddle until sugar dissolves. Add ice and bourbon or rye whiskey. Pour everything into a shaker glass, then back into the rocks glass. Garnish with another orange and/or cherry if desired. Bartending tip: You can choose to leave out the orange slice and cherry when muddling. You can also substitute a spoonful of simple syrup for the sugar cube and water.

WHEN YOU FEEL YOUNG

On the other side of things, did your school day make you feel like a kid again? Did a student ignite an immature fire in you when they blurted out something dumb and insulting? Did you have to fight the urge to dominate a kickball game at recess? Who knows your motivation, but if you're feeling young and frisky, you might want to fix yourself a spiked shirley temple later that day. Non-alcoholic alternative: Shirley Temple *(duh)*.

How to Make a Spiked Shirley Temple

Ice
1½ ounce vodka
½ ounce grenadine
4 ounces Sprite or ginger ale
Cherry, for serving

Fill a highball glass with ice. Combine all ingredients. Stir! Garnish with a cherry. Bartending tip: You can use as much or as little grenadine as you prefer. Actually, that goes for vodka too!

WHEN YOU ARE EXHAUSTED

Has it just been the longest day of your life? Was every student, staff member, and all of their mothers asking you for some kind of favor? Being a likeable and well-respected team player has its moments, but it can also be exhausting. Perk yourself up with a festive tequila sunrise, and start imagining summer break to spark up your sense of giving. Non-alcoholic alternative: Virgin Bay Breeze (made with pineapple and cranberry juice).

How to Make a Tequila Sunrise

Ice
1½ ounce tequila
3 ounces orange juice
½ ounce grenadine

Fill a highball glass with ice. Add tequila and orange juice. Drizzle grenadine into the glass. Bartending tip: Do not shake or stir! It's meant to look like a sunrise.

WHEN YOU ARE EMBARRASSED

It's only human that we embarrass ourselves at least twice a week. Did you blurt out an inappropriate word or have a weird slip of the tongue when addressing your class? Did you trip in the hallway or walk into a desk? No need to kill yourself; enjoy a delicious kamikaze instead. Non-alcoholic alternative: An entire bag of Doritos.

How to Make a Kamikaze Cocktail

Ice
1 ounce vodka
1 ounce triple sec
1 ounce lime juice
Lime wedge, for serving

Fill a cocktail shaker with ice. Add all ingredients. Shake! Strain into a chilled martini glass. Garnish with a lime.

WHEN YOUR THROAT HURTS

Everyone has a teacher voice. Is yours tired and winded? Maybe you had to raise your voice a bunch of times because your classroom was loud and boisterous. Maybe you are just weary of repeating instructions thirty million times. Try sipping on a warm hot toddy. That will soothe your pipes and give you the medicine you need to recover and sing a ballad of joy when starting your day tomorrow. Non-alcoholic alternative: Lemon-ginger herbal tea with honey.

How to Make a Hot Toddy

1½ ounce whiskey
½ ounce lemon juice
1 tablespoon honey
1 cup hot water

Combine all ingredients into a cute teacher mug. Stir gently. Bartending tip: Steep a black or green tea bag for an added kick.

WHEN YOU FEEL CRAZY

Okay, do not panic. It's totally normal that, on occasion, you feel like you have completely lost your mind. Actually, the conscious understanding that you feel insane means that you still hold a shred of sanity in the palm of your hand. The important thing is that you accept this as a reality and do not try to fight it. Instead, reach for a figurative representation of your brain with a Dark 'n' Stormy. If you are craving something lighter, an enormous tray of delicious brownies might do the trick.

How to Make a Dark 'n' Stormy

Ice
2 ounces dark rum
4 ounces ginger beer
Lime wedge, for serving

Fill a highball glass with ice. Combine dark rum and ginger beer. Stir gently. Bartending tip: Garnish with a lime wedge.

MIXING RESPONSIBILITY WITH RELAXATION

These pairings are connected in pure fun and aren't meant to take the place of other healthy alternatives and positive habits. They are a drink menu created with the intent of raising your spirits without lowering your inhibitions too much. (Okay, a little bit never hurt anybody.) As always, it's important to treat yourself to life's other good stuff and to keep a balance between what's good for your body and what's good for your soul. There's no need to be hard on yourself if you binge on a bunch of brownies one afternoon or if you have one too many glasses of wine at home. Give yourself a break, but balance that with a personal kick in your own rear when it's time to clean things up a bit. Nice dinners, frequent exercise, and at-home pampering techniques like bubble baths and facial masks are all ways to chill out in response to any of the aforementioned challenges and celebrations.

Teacher's Home Survival Kit

Boxes of wine: To wind down after all of the coffee.
Bubble bath: Because our bodies hurt all over.
Books: To keep our minds fresh.
TV: To give our minds a break.
Record player: To remind us of a simpler time.
Houseplants: To bring joy and life to Mondays.
Punching bag: Isn't it obvious?
Candles: To help us relax.
Tissues: Because sometimes we just need to cry.
Yoga mat: Because only heathens fall asleep on the bare floor.

Chapter 6

THE PERKS OF BEING A TEACHER

There's no doubt about it, teachers are planners. We have to be! We know more than most about how important it is to be organized and efficient. That doesn't just mean writing lesson plans, but also working hard at all of the elements that affect a child's life under our care at school. This includes creating a warm classroom environment, developing an organized method for productivity, and instilling policies and procedures that make our lives easier. We take great consideration when establishing a colorful backdrop for our teaching. We should put this same type of thought, creativity, and care into our personal lives.

"There is a scene in Billy Crystal's *City Slickers*, where he is talking about the 'one thing' that matters. It changes, and it is different every day. Sometimes, for me, it is taking time to be with family. Other times, it's about plugging in to the right thing and unplugging at the right time. I never go anywhere without my laptop or notepad. But I hate the word *survive*, and really strive to *thrive*."

—Mike, principal

MAKE IT COLORFUL

Most classrooms start out looking like a barren prison cell with zero personality. Bland and standard cement block walls line our existence. As if we need another reason to feel like we are two bad days away from an insane asylum! Instilling some life and color into the backdrop of where you work is essential for feeling happy and calm on a daily basis, and also for setting the tone for your students.

The same is true for our homes. Adding pops of color into your living space can bring a sense of vibrancy, fun, and energy. It also helps create a dynamic expression of how we feel. Some people believe there is a direct correlation between color and mood. Everyone is different, so colors may affect each person in a unique way. Typically, warm colors like red, yellow, and orange are associated with sparking energy while cool colors such as blue, green, and purple have a more calming effect. Vibrant shades of any color provide a nice contrast in small doses, while softer shades are less intimidating. Compromise can be a good thing. So, rather than painting an entire room a bright color, think about creating an accent wall or incorporating personality in the form of patterned wallpaper or unique décor, like pillows and picture frames.

MAKE IT FUNCTIONAL

In the classroom, it helps when our students know where to find things. That means less questions for us to answer, and more chances for them to put things back where they belong. At home, we may be more lenient with ourselves and become our own worst enemies in the process. What works in the classroom works in life, and vice versa. The more organized we are, the easier things become. The more we let things go, the harder it is to catch up. Think about the small things that will help make life run smoother.

DO YOUR HOMEWORK

Instead of waiting for the laundry to pile up like neglected homework, choose one weeknight to throw in just one load. That one wash per week may take a load off your weekend, when all you feel like doing is sitting around in clean sweatpants anyway.

PLAN AHEAD

Create a menu for the week rather than aimlessly roaming the grocery store, and don't shop hungry. Make it a habit of looking at what's on sale every Sunday, and build your grocery list off of that. Develop a rotation of go-to recipes that are easy and simple, and give yourself a break on the weekend when you don't feel like cooking.

STAY ORGANIZED

Keep all of your important documents, bills, and paperwork in a secure place in the house. Actually go through your mail and throw out the junk. Buy a paper shredder if you're worried about identity theft.

KEEP A RECORD

Write things down, but in the same place. Take note of food and living essentials when you use them up, so that the next time you are out, you know what you need.

Keep a calendar, chalkboard, or dry erase board on the wall. It's helpful to be able to see things written out as a reminder, and it will give you a platform to write sweet notes (or passive-aggressive ones) to the other people in your house!

KNOW WHAT YOU NEED

Clutter and mess can affect mood and even generate stress (more or less depending on your personality type). If you are a collector and not the type to let things go, buy yourself some plastic storage bins and, at the very least, put some of your stuff away and out of sight. You can do this seasonally, and then reassess your needs when it comes time to clean out the closet again.

MAKE IT INTENTIONAL

How might you incorporate your passion for teaching into your home's character? When decorating our classrooms and preparing for a new year, it can be fun and inspiring to incorporate some kind of theme into our planning. Pop-culture references, movie posters, musical interests, and hobbies are a good place to start. When you develop a theme for particular rooms in your house, it creates a fun work in progress that may take your mind off school. Think about how you can incorporate what you are passionate about into your home's design. What do you love? Whether it's the beach, the outdoors, buildings, architecture, art, history, books, sports, puppies, cars or coffee, anything can become a great foundation for building a particular style.

MAKE IT JOYFUL

Surround yourself with positive vibes both in the classroom and at home. Make your visual space so happy that it challenges you on a bad day. Give yourself the best shot at feeling like your best self. Print and frame inspirational quotes. Hang pictures of your favorite memories and most-loved people. Buy yourself flowers or plants. Breathe life into your living space by putting a piece of yourself into every piece of décor. The more character you create, the more you will feel at home. If a clean, crisp, and relatively empty house is reflective of your style, that's totally fine too! Let your home be a picture of who you are and what you like. It's all about making it more you. Creating a happy living space isn't just about what

we see, either. Play music that relaxes, inspires, or energizes you depending on your mood on any particular day. Burn candles or diffuse essential oils to make your home inviting. The more your home feels like "you," the more likely you will be able to relax and enjoy your time there.

Top Ten Ways to Spend a Personal Day

Hiding under a blanket
Bingeing your favorite TV show
Online shopping
Going to the gym
Hitting the beach
Organizing your closet
Meeting old friends for lunch
Reading a book
Pampering yourself with a massage or mani-pedi
Adopting a puppy

HOW TO CRAFT WORK-LIFE BALANCE

This lesson will encourage and invite teachers to recognize and respect professional boundaries that allow them to embrace and enjoy the good life.

DESCRIPTION

Developing and maintaining an ability to say no in spite of harboring an innate desire to save the world at all hours of the day and on weekends, while understanding and accepting that having a personal life and setting boundaries isn't a vocational sin.

OCCUPATIONAL AREAS

Childhood education, Self-care, Psychology, Compartmentalization, Personal care, Mental health, Physical health, Massage.

ADULT CONCEPTS

Teachers will understand how to:

- Realize that being happy at home translates into a more productive workday.
- Avoid burnout by prioritizing professional goals that suit and support a personal life.
- Draw a definitive line where the workday ends and the "me time" begins.
- Practice saying the words, "I'm sorry, I have an appointment," or "I have to run home to take out the dog," and other excuses in front of the staff bathroom mirror.
- Map out the best escape route to avoid conversational delays caused by friendly colleagues or talkative students.
- Identify professional catalysts for stress and acquire personal antidotes, such as bubble baths and punching bags.
- Differentiate between being a professional with boundaries, being an antisocial twerp who's difficult to work with, and just being lazy.

- Actually use a daily planner that was purchased at the beginning of the school year.
- Walk fast, hold papers, and stay focused to avoid talking to people in the hallway.
- Seek out a likable network of colleagues who share in the struggle, while politely avoiding overachievers or slackers who don't carry the same concept of balance.

LESSON OBJECTIVES

Teachers will be able to:

- Juggle ambition and realism without being too hard on themselves.
- Accept defeat and remember that failure is part of the process of being human. Tomorrow is another day.
- Say no when they realize they're already weary with too much on their plate.
- Carve out personal time to do something they enjoy, such as going for a run or reading a book.
- Choose productive strategies to complete tasks during off periods and lunch breaks to avoid bringing work home.
- Choose comfort over style when picking out shoes for the day.
- Decide that a store-made rotisserie chicken isn't too shabby of a dinner choice for a Monday (not to mention, it's affordable).
- Treat themselves to a new outfit or exciting mid-afternoon activity, such as eating ice cream or lying on the couch.
- Pour their heart into the school day without burning out by sundown.

SUPPLIES NEEDED

Calendar, Thousands of colorful Post-It notes, Back scratcher, Fast car, Yoga mat, Puppy, Luxurious bath salts, Patience, Pajamas, Security blanket.

ACTIVITIES

Teachers will:

- Prioritize themselves over being a martyr for others.
- Embrace their inner child for fun activities such as jumping on a trampoline.
- Ignore their inner child when faced with an acute desire to sarcastically insult a student.
- Breathe deeply between class periods.
- Accept the urge to savor a soggy sandwich and five seconds of peace during lunch, alone.
- Take advantage of benefits by enjoying a sick day for the sake of mental health.
- Work hard during contract hours so they don't feel guilty about not working 24/7.
- Make selective promises. Instead of doing everything, do a few things that matter and do them well.
- Make a list of professional and personal goals at the start of the school year.
- Don't criticize themselves if they don't actually meet all 10,000 of their goals.
- Have an internal conversation about how much they want to give and avoid comparing themselves to others who have different priorities.

EVALUATION

- Blood pressure
- Weight loss or gain
- Hunger
- Inner joy

"Teachers are shaping the future."
—*Nicole, teacher*

THE GOOD LIFE

The life of a teacher is a pretty good one. Our work completes us so long as we are mindful about molding ourselves alongside our duty to mold future generations. Just as it's important for us to be genuine and real with our students, we should be genuine and real with ourselves. Yes, we have plenty of things to take care of, but that list should include our own well-being. Most of us still carry the same creative spark and curiosity for knowledge we had as youngsters. Craving a break, a summer off, or a quality teacher perk doesn't make us selfish or lazy. It makes us smart—and we've earned it. We deserve to live the good life. A good life is a balanced one. A career in education offers job security while being a rewarding and inspiring vocation.

We have the opportunity to actually make a difference in the lives of others, and that responsibility is hard work. Our days are never boring. Forget about fortune-tellers. Teachers are the keepers of the future. We're on the front lines of tomorrow and we're on top of making it a better place. Our daily window into future generations gives us the chance to guide them in the right direction. Except, we're not just observing what comes next—we're facilitating it. That's why the world needs quality teachers, and that's why those quality teachers need to live the good life.

A teaching career is a marathon; the race is long but it's an accomplishment we won't ever forget. If we can finish without keeling over or pooping our pants, we have the confidence to know we are capable of conquering any challenge in our path. Fueled by ideals, ambition, and energy, we anticipate our place on the starting line for months. Sure, we have summer nightmares about it, but that's only because we care. Okay, it's also because we're tired and running on empty by the end. Who doesn't love the freedom of summer? It keeps us young. Throughout the school year, we're often low on gas and crawling to pit stops. We need help fueling our souls with the good stuff. That balance helps us pace our students through the school year in a lasting and positive way. There are lulls in the rat race of teaching and miles where we require a cheerful reassurance that we can do it. We can make it, and we're in this arduous journey together.

After all, teaching is a fast-paced job. It's a workout that requires mental stamina, but it's not a sprint. First-year teachers might be peeing their pants, figuratively, and hopefully not literally. Passionate veteran teachers who should have retired years ago may be battling an incontinence problem. (We all know the ones who would prefer to crawl to school in a walker before accepting a retirement plan.) Forget

about that sweet pension, there's still important work to be done! Meanwhile, some of us are over here counting down the days until we can hit the beach all year long.

It doesn't matter if teachers are on a break; they never stop teaching. The duties of the job mold themselves into our DNA like a genetics experiment. No matter how hard we fight the urge to correct or help others outside of school, we feel compelled to continue making a difference. (Okay, maybe correcting grammar on social media isn't making that much of a difference, but it makes us feel better.) There's an unspoken oath we take when becoming teachers. We have a respon-sibility to be our best selves, not just at school, but all of the time. Hey—not all superheroes wear capes. Some of us are in cardigans and loafers. Sure, we can all try to turn off our minds, but this work is in our soul and it's not going anywhere. When that last bell rings, we're still teachers and the work doesn't end. We're thinking about it. We're brainstorming new ideas. We're reminded of our students or something funny that happened during class, and we're smiling in spite of being oh so very tired.

We don't stop being teachers on the weekends even if we do dive behind a bunch of bananas to hide from our students at the supermarket. We may not be as patient with our loved ones as we are with our students, but that's because we only have so much to give and we use up a lot of our friendly voices at school. We put on an unbreakable façade, but on the inside, we're fighting to keep our optimism fresh and strong. It's hard to fully understand the life of a teacher until you've lived the life of a teacher. The outside world supports and encourages us. They even give us sweet discounts, but not everyone understands the chaos of a teacher. We have learned how to manage mayhem like strategic negotiators. We can become so good at juggling everything that students, parents, and administrators forget we aren't actually blessed with superpowers.

"I think it is also challenging when people who have never stepped foot in a classroom are making decisions on education. I challenge those who think, 'Anyone can teach,' to spend a day in a classroom."

–Casey, teacher

This is tough work, and sometimes in spite of all of the work we put into a particular effort, we don't feel like we are getting anywhere. We keep moving along that marathon trail anyway. Most of us have an annoying ability to sense the light at the end of the tunnel, even if it's through the gaze of tear-filled or bloodshot eyeballs. It's not just tough waking up in the wee hours of the morning and doing our best to generate the energy required to field thirty questions before lunch. Lunch hour, by the way, is usually before noon. Second lunch comes after school when we're starving for a nap and some sustenance to keep us alive until dinner.

We do our best to recharge our batteries on the drive home by listening to music or doing some kind of breathing exercise. It's awesome that we miss rush hour and can be on our merry way before the rest of those nine-to-fivers, but we must actively fight the urge to spend some of our bonus hours in a catatonic state.

The tendency of blindly losing ourselves in a stare contest with the living room wall feels like a daily rite of passage. We wonder how we will ever make it to dinner without dying first. If only we could put some unfinished work under our pillows and have it magically completed by morning—maybe then we can actually rest in peace.

There are some days when we can do it all. There are other trying (and maybe crying) times when we think we can barely tie our shoes, let alone write a lesson plan or corral a classroom of twenty children. In spite of this, we all continue to show up—and we love our jobs. We have a pretty sweet schedule, especially during the summer months, and we've got some great perks. Except, those aren't the only reasons we keep doing this. There's a more powerful truth driving our mission. The reasons may be different for all of us.

"I decided to become a teacher during my senior year of high school. There were so many teachers who made an impact on me that I decided to try and be that to others."

—*Nicole, teacher*

Maybe you were inspired to follow in the footsteps of a former teacher who made a real connection. Perhaps you felt disappointed in your own educational experience as a child, and you became determined to grow up and make it better. Some of us are lifelong learners who lived for philosophical conversations we held in the classroom. We teach because we have an innate desire to keep learning ourselves while we forge a new role in the system.

"There is a feeling, and it is hard to explain, that only comes every so often, after a certain assignment, when a student perseveres, when the work is recognized. There is nothing quite like that, and it sustains through really difficult times. Also, as a principal, I get to learn from and interact with literally hundreds of folks, which means I get to be in a constant evolution as a learner – which is awesome."

—*Mike, principal*

For some of us, and maybe all of us, it wasn't just about making a difference in the lives of children and the future of society. It wasn't just about having the summers off. It was about giving ourselves the best chance to lead a balanced, beautiful, and overall fulfilling life. Whether you are a new teacher or have been doing this for decades, the connection between all of us remains the same. Our style of teaching might change with the times and new technology, but every teacher shares some kind of vision for leaving the world better than we found it. Let's use that inspirational technique to do our best to ensure each day we live is better than yesterday. We're teachers—let's live the good life as we help build a better tomorrow.

Top Ten Songs to Kick Off Summer
School's Out by Alice Cooper
All Summer Long by Kid Rock
Margaritaville by Jimmy Buffet
Summertime by DJ Jazzy Jeff & The Fresh Prince
The Boys of Summer by Don Henley
Summer in the City by the Lovin' Spoonful
Here Comes the Sun by the Beatles
Walking on Sunshine by Katrina and the Waves
Paradise City by Guns n' Roses
Dog Days are Over by Florence and the Machine

About the Author

Melanie J. Pellowski graduated Phi Beta Kappa from Rutgers University in 2005 with a major in American studies and minors in mathematics and theatre arts. Her passion for learning and storytelling inspired her to pursue a master's degree in journalism from Boston University, which she earned in 2008. While she spent nearly a decade working various roles as a multimedia journalist, digital host, reporter, and producer, much of her stories involved visiting schools and interviewing students. After reporting on Rhode Island high school sports and producing human-interest features on Division I athletics, Melanie felt compelled to find her way back to the classroom. A desire to balance a rewarding full-time job with a well-rounded personal life and the time to focus on writing led her to pursue the possibility of becoming a teacher.

Since then, Melanie has helped build an educational television production program that teaches high school students what it's like to work in a professional TV studio. Her classes produce content for a weekly morning show that highlights positive news happening in their school community. Becoming a teacher has helped her find a happy medium between continuing to pursue her own creative goals while helping future generations of storytellers find their own unique paths. After realizing teaching was the most challenging, exhausting, and rewarding job she has ever undertaken, she was inspired to find a balance and help other teachers do the same. She writes under her maiden name, Pellowski, but her students know her as Mrs. LaPlaca. She has a tremendous amount of respect for fellow teachers, colleagues, and friends who work in education. Melanie has written *The Teacher's Guide to Self-Care* with these hard-working, good-hearted people in mind. Look for Melanie's other works published by Skyhorse Publishing, including *My Dearest Bridesmaid, My Dearest Sister*, and *The Pregnancy Primer*.

Acknowledgments

This book was inspired by generations of well-rounded educators who see the bigger picture in teaching life skills to students, but also the importance of putting value into their own passions, interests, and lives outside of work. Thank you to Casey, Corrin, Kristen, Jen, Mike, and Nicole, the friends and colleagues who were kind enough to provide their own perspectives in the form of insightful thoughts and anecdotes. I would not even have the perspective to write this book had my Practical Arts supervisor, Doug, not seen my professional background in journalism and broadcasting as a useful tool for enhancing a high school television program and giving me the opportunity to make a transition into teaching. Hopewell Valley Regional School District fosters not only creative learning and growth for its student body, but also encourages professional staff to become better people, inspiring me to remain versatile and motivated in all avenues of life.

Thank you to my father, Michael, for suggesting I consider a career move to education after discussing my overall goals for life in general. To my mother, Judith, for being so supportive and thoughtful through college and graduate school. To my brothers, Morgan, Matthew, and Martin, for teaching me to be creatively driven, and to my husband, Nicholas, for believing I would make a great teacher. To my nieces and nephews, Skyeler, Hannah, Loukas, and Ethan, for inspiring me to care about the future of education. Finally—thank you to Nicole Mele and Skyhorse Publishing for making the publication of *The Teacher's Guide* possible.

Bibliography

"9 Benefits and Uses of Oregano Oil." Healthline. Accessed December 2019. https://www.healthline.com/nutrition/9-oregano-oil-benefits-and-uses.

"10 Uses for Lemon Essential Oil." Mighty Nest. June 8, 2016. https://mightynest.com/articles/10-uses-for-lemon-essential-oil.

"11 Benefits of Tea Tree Oil." Medical News Today. Accessed December 2019. https://www.medicalnewstoday.com/articles/262944.php.

"12 Top Essential Oils and Their Uses (60+ Tips and Ideas)." Organixx. Accessed December 2019. https://organixx.com/essential-oils-and-their-uses/.

"About Peppermint Oil Uses and Benefits." Healthline. Accessed December 2019. https://www.healthline.com/health/benefits-of-peppermint-oil.

"All About Oregano Essential Oil." New Directions Aromatics. Accessed December 2019. https://www.newdirectionsaromatics.com/blog/products/all-about-oregano-oil.html.

Bradford, Alina. "The Five (and More) Senses." Live Science. Accessed December 2019. https://www.livescience.com/60752-human-senses.html.

Britt, Robert Roy. "Can Exercise Make You Happy? Or Does Happiness Help You Exercise?" Luminate. January 28, 2019.

Cherney, K. and Tim Jewell. "Alcohol and Anxiety." Healthline. November 30, 2016. https://www.healthline.com/health/alcohol-and-anxiety.

Cherry, Kendra. "Color Psychology: Does It Affect How You Feel?" Very Well Mind. July 17, 2019. https://www.verywellmind.com/color-psychology-2795824.

Cooper, Ellen. "Top 15 Most Popular Essential Oils to Start With: Uses and Benefits." August 12, 2019. https://aromatalking.com/most-popular-essential-oils/.

"Developmental Milestones: Touch." BabyCentre UK. Accessed December 2019. https://www.babycentre.co.uk/a25012711/developmental-milestones-touch.

Ducharme, Jamie. "Spending Just 20 Minutes in a Park Makes You Happier. Here's What Else Being Outside Can Do for Your Health." Time. February 28, 2019. https://time.com/5539942/green-space-health-wellness/.

"Essential Oils for Hangovers." Eco Modern Essentials. December 11, 2018. https://ecomodernessentials.com.au/blogs/eco-modern-essentials-blog /essential-oils-for-hangovers.

"Essential Oils in the Ancient World, Part I." The Lavender Life. *Young Living.* Accessed December 2019. https://www.youngliving.com/blog/essential-oils -in-the-ancient-world-pt-i/.

"Essential Oils in the Ancient World, Part II." The Lavender Life. *Young Living.* Accessed December 2019. https://www.youngliving.com/blog/essential-oils -in-the-ancient-world-part-ii/.

"Essential Oils in the Ancient World: Part III." The Lavender Life. *Young Living.* Accessed December 2019. https://www.youngliving.com/blog/essential-oils -in-the-ancient-world-part-iii/.

"Essential Oil: Plant Substance." Britannica. Accessed December 2019. https: //www.britannica.com/topic/essential-oil.

"FDA Regulation of Essential Oils." Aromatherapy: Clinical Use of Essential Oils. *University of Minnesota.* Accessed December 2019. https://www.coursera. org/lecture/aromatherapy-clinical-use-essential-oils/fda-regulation-of -essential-oils-1eBtl.

Fetters, K. Aleisha. "10 Benefits of Swimming that Will Have You Diving into the Pool." Shape. January 2, 2020. https://www.shape.com/fitness/workouts/ benefits-of-swimming.

Godman, Heidi. "Regular Exercise Changes the Brain to Improve Memory, Thinking Skills." Harvard Health Publishing. April 9, 2014. https://www. health.harvard.edu/blog/regular-exercise-changes-brain-improve-memory- thinking-skills-201404097110.

Gremillion, Allison S. "Colors and Emotions: How Colors Make You Feel." 99 Designs. Accessed December 2019. https://99designs.com/blog/tips/ how-color-impacts-emotions-and-behaviors/.

"History of Essential Oils." Essential Oils Academy. Accessed December 2019. http://essentialoilsacademy.com/history/.

"History of Essential Oils." FGB Natural Products. Accessed December 2019. https://www.fgb.com.au/content/history-essential-oils.

Holcombe, Kate. "Breathe Easy: Relax with Pranayama." Yoga Journal. April 12, 2017. https://www.yogajournal.com/practice/healing-breath.

"International Bartenders Association." Accessed December 2019. https://iba-world.com/.

Keltner, Dacher. "Hands On Research: The Science of Touch." Greater Good Magazine. UC Berkley. September 29, 2010. https://greatergood.berkeley.edu/article/item/hands_on_research.

Luna, Aletheia. "The Ultimate Guide to Crown Chakra Healing for Complete Beginners." Lonerwolf. Accessed December 2019. https://lonerwolf.com/crown-chakra-healing/.

Luna, Aletheia. "The Ultimate Guide to Heart Chakra Healing for Complete Beginners." Lonerwolf. Accessed December 2019. https://lonerwolf.com/heart-chakra-healing/.

Luna, Aletheia. "The Ultimate Guide to Root Chakra Healing for Complete Beginners." Lonerwolf. Accessed December 2019. https://lonerwolf.com/root-chakra-healing/.

Luna, Aletheia. "The Ultimate Guide to Sacral Chakra Healing for Complete Beginners." Lonerwolf. Accessed December 2019. https://lonerwolf.com/sacral-chakra-healing/.

Luna, Aletheia. "The Ultimate Guide to Solar Plexus Chakra Healing for Complete Beginners." Lonerwolf. Accessed December 2019. https://lonerwolf.com/solar-plexus-chakra-healing/.

Luna, Aletheia. "The Ultimate Guide to Third Eye Chakra Healing for Complete Beginners." Lonerwolf. Accessed December 2019. https://lonerwolf.com/third-eye-chakra-healing/.

Luna, Aletheia. "The Ultimate Guide to Throat Chakra Healing for Complete Beginners." Lonerwolf. Accessed December 2019. https://lonerwolf.com/throat-chakra-healing/.

McCulloch, Marsha, MS, RD. "14 Benefits and Uses of Rosemary Essential Oil." Healthline. November 15, 2018. https://www.healthline.com/nutrition/rosemary-oil-benefits.

Reynolds, Gretchen. "Even a Little Exercise Might Make Us Happier." The New York Times. May 2, 2018. https://www.nytimes.com/2018/05/02/well/move/even-a-little-exercise might-make-us-happier.html.

Rodriguez, T., Tracy Middleton and Korin Miller. "The 15 Best Essential Oils for Aromatherapy—And How to Use Them." Women's Health. December 10, 2019. https://www.womenshealthmag.com/health/a19904702/essential-oils/.

"The Secret to Better Health – Exercise." Harvard Health Publishing. Harvard Medical School. Accessed December 2019. https://www.health.harvard.edu/healthbeat/the-secret-to-better-health-exercise.

"Special Senses: Taste (Gustation)." Lumen Learning. Accessed December 2019. https://courses.lumenlearning.com/austincc-ap1/chapter/special-senses-taste-gustation/.

Specktor, Brandon. "The Brilliant Reason Wet Fingers Prune Up (And 6 Other Secrets About Your Sense of Touch)." The Healthy. February 9, 2017. https://www.thehealthy.com/mental-health/sense-touch-facts/.

Stinson, Annakeara. "Essential Oils That Make You Dream, If You're Looking to Spice Up Your Snooze." Elite Daily. November 3, 2017. https://www.elitedaily.com/p/essential-oils-that-make-you-dream-if-youre-looking-to-spice-up-your-snooze-3217651.

Wallace, Dillon. "Memories: Which Sense is the Strongest?" Southtree. Accessed December 2019. https://southtree.com/blogs/artifact/memories-which-sense-is-the-strongest.

"What Are Essential Oils, and Do They Work?" Healthline. Accessed December 2019. https://www.healthline.com/nutrition/what-are-essential-oils.

"What are the Health Benefits and Risk of Lavender?" Medical News Today. Accessed December 2019. https://www.medicalnewstoday.com/articles/265922.php.

"What Is Aromatherapy and How Does It Help Me?" Healthline. Accessed December 2019. https://www.healthline.com/health/what-is-aromatherapy.

Widrich, Leo. "What Happens to Our Brains When We Exercise and How It Makes Us Happier." Fast Company. February 4, 2014. https://www.fastcompany.com/3025957/what-happens-to-our-brains-when-we-exercise-and-how-it-makes-us-happier.

Winter, Catherine. "10 Essential Oils to Always Have at Home." Lifehack. Accessed December 2019. https://www.lifehack.org/articles/lifestyle/10-essential-oils-always-have-home.html.

Zaraska, Marta. "The Sense of Smell in Humans is More Powerful Than We Think." Discover Magazine. October 11, 2017. https://www.discovermagazine.com/mind/the-sense-of-smell-in-humans-is-more-powerful-than-we-think.

Notes

....

....

....

....

....

....

....

....

....

....

....

....

....

....

....

Notes

....

....

....

....

....

....

....

....

....

....

....

....

....

....

# Notes

....

....

....

....

....

....

....

....

....

....

....

....

....

....

....

Notes

....

....

....

....

....

....

....

....

....

....

....

....

....

....

....

....

Notes

....

....

....

....

....

....

....

....

....

....

....

....

....

....

....

Notes

....
....
....
....
....
....
....
....
....
....
....
....
....
....
....

Notes

....

....

....

....

....

....

....

....

....

....

....

....

....

....

....

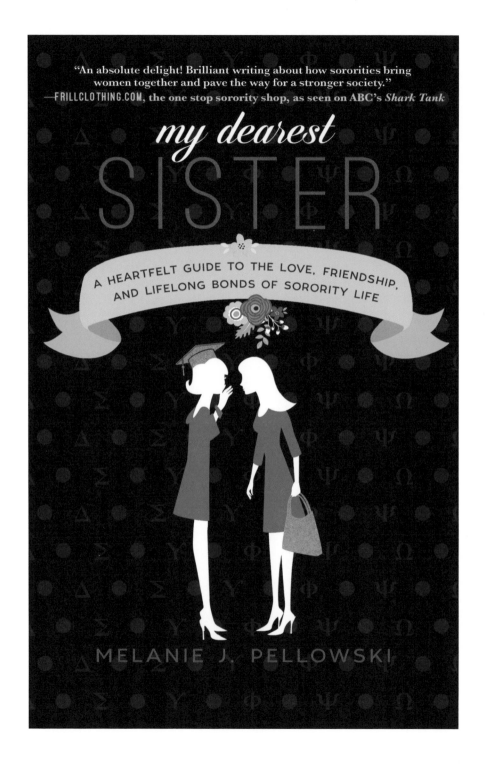

my dearest
SISTER

A HEARTFELT GUIDE TO THE LOVE, FRIENDSHIP, AND LIFELONG BONDS OF SORORITY LIFE

MELANIE J. PELLOWSKI

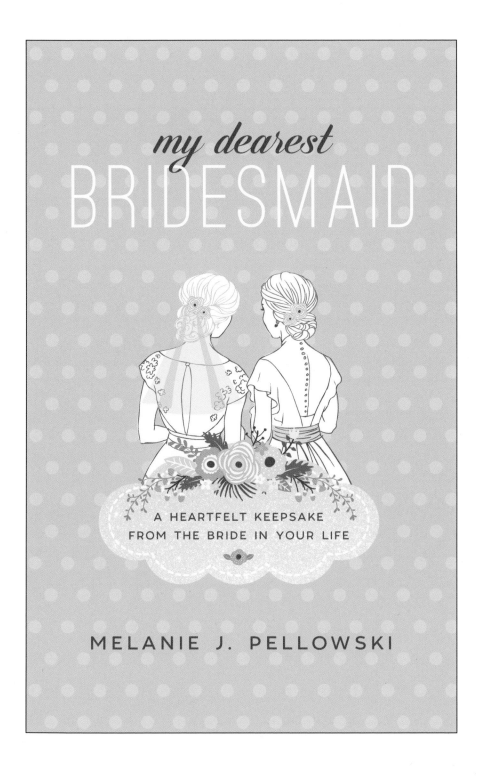

my dearest
BRIDESMAID

A HEARTFELT KEEPSAKE
FROM THE BRIDE IN YOUR LIFE

MELANIE J. PELLOWSKI